F. F. BRUCE

PAUL & HIS CONVERTS

How Paul
Nurtured the
Churches
He Planted

INTERVARSITY PRESS
DOWNERS GROVE, ILLINOIS 60515

Published in the United States of America by InterVarsity Press, Downers Grove, Illinois, with permission from Highland Books, a division of Edward England Books, East Sussex, England. The original edition from which this was revised and expanded was published in 1962.

InterVarsity Press is the book-publishing division of Inter-Varsity Christian Fellowship, a student movement active on campus at hundreds of universities, colleges and schools of nursing. For information about local and regional activities, write IVCF, 233 Langdon St., Madison, WI 53703.

Distributed in Canada through InterVarsity Press, 860 Denison St., Unit 3, Markham, Ontario L3R 4H1, Canada.

Cover illustration: Roberta Polfus

ISBN 0-87784-593-X

Printed in the United States of America

Library of Congress Cataloguing in Publication Data
Bruce, F. F. (Frederick Fyvie), 1910-
Paul and his converts.

1. Bible. N.T. Thessalonians—Criticism, interpretation, etc. 2. Bible. N.T. Corinthians—Criticism, interpretation, etc. 3. Bible. N.T. Philippians—Criticism, interpretation, etc.
4. Paul, the Apostle, Saint.
I. Title.
BX2725.2.B7   1985   227   85-19764
ISBN 0-87784-593-X

| 18 | 17 | 16 | 15 | 14 | 13 | 12 | 11 | 10 | 9 | 8 | 7 | 6 | 5 | 4 | 3 | 2 | 1 |
| 99 | 98 | 97 | 96 | 95 | 94 | 93 | 92 | 91 | 90 | 89 | 88 | 87 | 86 | 85 | | | |

To Raymond and Florence Payne

Preface

This work was originally issued in 1962 as one of a paperback series of twenty-two Bible Guides, edited by the late William Barclay and myself and published by the Lutterworth Press. The series has served its generation and it is not proposed to reissue it.

According to the plan of that series, this volume dealt with Paul's letters to the Thessalonians and the Corinthians. The text has now been revised and the work has been expanded so as to take in the letter to the Philippians as well. It thus serves as an introductory handbook to the whole of Paul's surviving correspondence with his converts in Europe.

Eastertide, 1984   F.F.B.

Introduction

In this handbook we are to look at five of the earliest Christian writings that have been preserved to us: the First and Second Letters to the Thessalonians, the First and Second Letters to the Corinthians, and the Letter to the Philippians. (They are put here in the order in which they were written, rather than the order in which they appear in most editions of the New Testament.)

These letters were sent by Paul the apostle to his converts in three important cities of the Macedonian and Greek provinces of the Roman Empire. They were written between the early fifties and early sixties of the first century A.D.—that is to say, some twenty to thirty years after the death of Christ. At that time hundreds of people were still alive who had vivid recollections of seeing Christ and listening to his words. Documents of this kind, written so soon after the inception of a new religious movement, have a high historical value. To Christians, however, their value is not only historical; they help us immensely to understand the faith which we hold, and which from time to time we are called upon to defend.

The New Testament presents us with the foundation documents of our faith, and among these foundation documents the letters of Paul are of unique interest and importance. As we read them, we are impressed by the way in which basic problems recur from age to age. In spite of the vast cultural differences between Paul's day and ours, the Christian mission today faces situations not essentially different from those which confronted Paul, and the younger churches of the twentieth century pass through experiences with which the young churches of the first century were well acquainted. Indeed, a great missionary statesman of the earlier part of this century, Roland Allen (author of *Missionary Methods: St. Paul's or Ours?*), argued powerfully that Paul's missionary policy is the policy best adapted to our own times. At any rate, both for the strategy to be followed in the propagation of the gospel, and for the problems of personal Christian life and the witness of Christian communities in a non-Christian environment, Paul has words of wisdom for us today which it would be foolish to disregard.

This handbook is intended to give help in the study of the books with which it deals, not to be a substitute for their study. It would be a good idea to read the five letters through fairly quickly before starting to use this work, and then read them through again, section by section, along with it. The version here used is the Revised Standard Version. It would be helpful to have one or two other versions handy for comparison, such as the New English Bible, the New International

Version, or the Good News Bible. But, for a rapid preliminary reading of these and other letters of Paul, perhaps the most illuminating version is J. B. Phillips's paraphrase, *The New Testament in Modern English*.

1
Paul and His Letters

"Letters to young churches"

THERE ARE twenty-seven documents—"books",
we commonly call them—in the New Testament.
Twenty-one of these are letters, written occasionally to
individuals but more often to churches or Christian
communities. Of these twenty-one letters, thirteen
bear the name of Paul as their writer. Of these thirteen,
nine fall into the category of what J. B. Phillips called
"Letters to young churches"; they were addressed, that
is to say, to newly-founded churches whose members
were quite recent and inexperienced converts to Christianity. Most of those churches had been founded by
Paul himself; their members had been converted to
Christianity through his powerful presentation of the
gospel. When he writes to them he is like a father
addressing his children. He cannot conceal the strength
and warmth of his affection for them, he commends
everything that is praiseworthy in them (where others
might have found little enough to commend), he

scolds them for their shortcomings, he warns them that if they do not mend their ways he will take a big stick with him next time he comes to see them, he encourages them for all he is worth, and makes no secret of his consuming desire that they should grow up to be hundred-per-cent Christians, worthy of the honourable name which they bear.

Paul's world significance

Paul is one of the most significant figures in the history of civilization. To him, far more than to any other person, is due the direction which Christianity took in the first generation after the death and resurrection of Jesus. It is interesting at times (if not very fruitful) to speculate on the might-have-beens of history. What might have been the course of Christianity had Paul never become a Christian? Would it have remained one among several movements within the frontiers of Judaism? Would it have remained a predominantly Asian religion, like other great movements which originated in the same continent? So we might go on, asking questions whose only value is to emphasize the significance of the life and work of Paul.

Today, over wide areas of the earth, Christianity is regarded as primarily a European religion (for this purpose, "European" includes "American"). Whereas that may once have been looked upon as an advantage, nowadays it is a handicap to be overcome. But if it be asked how a faith which arose in Asia should have come to be so universally associated with European civilization, the answer to the question must be sought in the life and activity of Paul. In the providence of God, the leading herald of the Christian message during the first three decades of the apostolic age was a Roman citizen, who saw how the strategic centres and communications of the Roman Empire could be exploited in the interests of the kingdom of Christ, and planted the faith in those centres and along those lines of communication. By launching the gospel within the principal provinces of the Roman Empire, Paul ensured that it would continue to advance more and more widely over the empire. At last the Roman Empire, with its rich heritage of Greek culture and Roman law and organization, was won for Christianity, and Christianity has been a dominant element in this heritage ever since. For European civilization has never ceased to be in essence the civilization bequeathed by the christianized Roman Empire.

Or we might ask another interesting historical question. Since Christianity began as a movement within the commonwealth of Israel, how is it that, less than a century after its inception, it presented the appearance of a mainly Gentile faith? The answer to this question too lies in the effectiveness of the ministry of Paul as the divinely chosen apostle to the Gentiles. Some Gentiles indeed had been converted to Christianity before Paul was fairly launched upon his apostolic career, but it was he above all others who carried the gospel throughout the Gentile lands. He regarded his apostleship as a priestly service, in which the conversion of the Gentiles was the acceptable sacrifice which he desired to present to God. It gave him no joy to see the Jews so reluctant to accept the gospel, while Gentiles flocked to enjoy its blessings; he hoped indeed that the spectacle of the inexhaustible gospel blessings enjoyed by Gentiles would one day incite the Jews to emulate them and claim their own ancestral share in those blessings. But since his personal task was the evangelization of Gentiles, he devoted himself to it, with results that are plain for all to read.

The gospel and the Gentiles

When the gospel was presented to Jewish hearers, or to Gentiles who already had an attachment to the Jewish religion and way of life, the preacher could take it for granted that his hearers believed in one God, the creator of the world, a righteous and merciful God, who desired his people to be righteous and merciful too, and had given them his law for the guidance of their lives. But in the course of his ministry to Gentiles, Paul often found himself confronted by hearers whose religious and ethical background was quite different from that. They were idolaters, worshipping many gods who in fact were no gods. While they acknowledged standards of right and wrong, many of them would have confessed that this acknowledgement was largely a matter of lip service; and in some departments of life, notably in relations between the sexes, even the standards which they acknowledged were far laxer than those which the Jewish law and the Christian gospel alike maintained.

To such pagan audiences Paul had to speak first of

all about the true God, who had made heaven and earth and everything in them, who gave them all good things—life and food and everything else—for their rich enjoyment. This God, he said, had never left himself without a witness in the world, but now he had acted decisively for men's salvation by sending his Son Jesus Christ into the world. The coming of Christ was not unforeseen, for the prophets of Israel in earlier days had foretold it. They also foretold that he would give up his life as an offering to God for the sins of men, and that he would be raised from the dead. This had actually taken place, for Christ was crucified, and on the third day thereafter he rose from the grave and was seen by many witnesses. To their testimony Paul could add his own; he too, long after the others, had seen the risen Christ for himself. And through this Christ, crucified and risen, God was now offering his great salvation to all who placed their faith in him. The word "salvation" at least was not strange to these Gentiles; it spoke of that release from the burden of guilt and the fear of death which many of them were seeking fruitlessly in those days.

Paul was a bold man to offer them a *crucified* Saviour. For crucifixion was not only an unspeakably agonizing form of death; it was also utterly shameful. To die on a cross was to plumb the lowest depths of disgrace. Could self-respecting and intelligent people really be expected to trust in a *crucified* Saviour? Paul knew that his gospel of Christ crucified seemed folly to the Greeks, but he persisted in placing Christ crucified in the forefront of his preaching. And the event proved him right, for great numbers of his hearers did place their faith in this crucified Saviour, and found new life and new power in doing so. They exulted in their conscious deliverance from spiritual bondage and oppression. That the Spirit of God had taken possession of their lives was to them no mere verbiage; it was a real experience.

A *new way of life*

But what were these people to be told about the way of life which they ought to live from now on? And how could they be expected to overcome their former habits and resist the pull of their immoral and idolatrous environments? Paul reminds his converts at Corinth that some of them were formerly "immoral, idolaters, adulterers, homosexuals, thieves, greedy, drunkards, revilers, robbers" (1 Corinthians 6:9f.). What was the best way to teach such people the rudiments of sound morality?

Most of the Christians back home in Jerusalem would have said there was only one way; these people must be taught the law of Moses and told that unless they keep that law in addition to believing in Christ there is no salvation for them. But Paul could not do this. He had learned in his own experience that all the law-keeping in the world could never bring assurance of salvation and peace with God—and he knew more about law-keeping than most of his critics did. But the moment he surrendered his life to Christ he knew that he had found the true way of salvation and peace. And he contended that when a man yielded himself to the living Christ and the power of his Spirit, his inward being was so changed that, from that time forth, he delighted to produce spontaneously "the fruit of the Spirit", those graces which were to be seen in their harmonious perfection in the life of Christ.

Many Christians thought that Paul was being impossibly optimistic. This conception, they said, might work all right with people who already had a stable moral foundation, but how could it work with a crowd of immoral pagans such as had been swept into some of Paul's Gentile churches? Could it work in Philippi and Thessalonica? Above all, could it work in Corinth? The very name of Corinth was a byword for immorality throughout a pagan world that was none too particular. Paul maintained that it could work, even among people whose background and environment were so unpromising: and in the long run Paul's way was vindicated. But at the time many of his friends (not to speak of his opponents) seriously thought that he was lowering the ethical standards of the gospel through his laxity. And in justification of their criticism they could point to some sad lapses among Paul's converts.

Paul deplored these lapses as much as his critics did—more so, in fact. For he knew that his apostolic reputation was bound up with his converts' behaviour —his apostolic reputation not so much in the eyes of men as in the sight of God. Repeatedly he tells his converts that he can look forward with confidence to the day when he must give an account of his stewardship before the tribunal of Christ only if they stand firm in their faith and prove the genuineness of their Christianity by the quality of their lives. But he treats them as mature sons of God; instead of imposing a code of rules on them he sets before them the perfect standard of Christ—Christ not merely as an external example but Christ being reproduced within them by the power of the Spirit.

This is a higher standard than the best-devised of law codes. He calls it "the law of Christ" (1 Corinthians 9:21), but it is a law written in men's hearts and not on stone or parchment. It is a law which forbids Christians to live irregular lives, to quarrel with one another, to interfere in other people's business, to live at other people's expense when they are perfectly able to earn their own living. But it is not in essence a negative law, telling people what not to do (as most of the Ten Commandments did); it is the positive law of Christian love. Jesus had summed up the Old Testament law in two great commandments: "Thou shalt love the LORD thy God with all thy heart" (Deuteronomy 6:5) and "Thou shalt love thy neighbour as thyself" (Leviticus 19:18). But he had done more than that: his whole life had embodied this law of love and provided his followers with a standard for their own emulation. When Paul, in 1 Corinthians 13, sings his hymn in praise of heavenly love, he celebrates love very largely in personal terms; it has often been pointed out that one might replace the word "love" in that chapter by the name of Christ and have a faithful portrait of his character. And if the power of the indwelling Spirit of

22

God reproduced this character of Christ in the lives of his people, then they would spontaneously follow the law of love. This was Paul's ambition for his converts.

It was no easy way that he chose, but it was incomparably the noblest way, and he never doubted that it was the only right way for men and women who had come of age spiritually through faith in Christ. It was a way that brought him disappointment time and again, as his converts failed to rise to "the upward call of God in Christ Jesus" (Philippians 3:14). But it never brought him disillusionment; his many disappointments were more than matched by the readiness with which other converts of his—some of them newly liberated from idolatry—embraced his teaching and exhibited the Christ-likeness in their lives, shining like bright lights in an environment of spiritual and ethical darkness. Converts like these confirmed him in his conviction that his high ideal was the proper ideal to set before them, and he encouraged them untiringly to go on as they had begun.

Fighting on two fronts

It is this note of encouragement that we can hear above all others in his letters to the churches of Thessalonica, Corinth and Philippi. The situation in the Corinthian church was a specially delicate one for him to tackle, as he found it necessary to fight simultaneously on two fronts. There were not only those members of the church who thought that the gospel released them from all ethical convention; there were others who (partly, no doubt, by way of reaction to these) went to the opposite extreme and tried, in the name of Christianity, to set up various taboos. Some of them thought that the married state was unfit for Christians; some wished to ban certain kinds of food, and so forth. So, while Paul was doing all he could, on the one hand, to restrain those who misinterpreted Christian liberty to mean licence to do anything they chose, he was obliged to deal firmly, on the other hand, with those who wanted to introduce a new set of prohibitions which would have banished Christian liberty altogether.

We have to bear all this in mind if we are to understand the arguments he employs now on this side and now on that. He tried to go as far as he could with both sides, until the point came where he had to stand fast and vindicate the principles of the gospel. He agreed with much that the libertarians said about Christian freedom, but reminded them of the responsibilities which that freedom carried with it. He agreed with much that the ascetic party said about self-denial —after all, he practised self-denial far beyond what they did—but he insisted that self-denial must be a voluntary discipline, not to be imposed on others against their will, and not to be imposed on oneself in a spirit of legalism or with the idea that this was a way to acquire special merit in God's sight. To the one group he said, "Liberty, not licence"; to the other he said, "Liberty, not bondage". The people to whom he wrote were Christians, living in a non-Christian environment; they should therefore remember that the public reputation of Christianity, and indeed of Christ himself, depended on their behaviour. But there was an even higher incentive than that: they should remember above all that they were called to please Christ. To win Christ's approval mattered supremely in his converts' lives. To this end, then, he gave them every encouragement.

Gentile churches in a pagan environment

What were the features which distinguished a Pauline church and its members from the surrounding world? Members of a Jewish community in a pagan city were distinguished in a variety of ways: the males among them were all circumcised, they all desisted from ordinary work on the weekly sabbath and observed other special days in their sacred calendar, they abstained from some kinds of food which their neighbours ate as a matter of course. But Paul refused to have any of these distinguishing features imposed on his Gentile converts: no one must imagine that they must first become Jews before they could be Christians.

For his own part, Paul speaks of the cross of Christ as forming a barrier or fence between him and the world: that is probably what he means when he says that by the cross "the world has been crucified to me, and I to the world" (Galatians 6:14). What Paul calls "the word of the cross" (1 Corinthians 1:18) was as determinant for his way of life as for his gospel preaching and what this meant for him in practice can be discovered from a study of his writings. He presented his own example in this respect for the imitation of his converts, but it had to be worked out differently for them. Paul moved on from one place to another, but most of his converts stayed in one place all their lives.

In the cities where they lived they were already members of social groups. They had their families, their neighbours, their fellow-workers. From none of these were they required to cut themselves off. If their former associates disowned them or would have nothing to do with them, that could not be helped; otherwise, former associations were to be maintained. Their maintenance, indeed, might provide missionary opportunities. The converted husband was not to give up living with his pagan wife if she was content to go on living with him. The converted wife was not to leave her pagan husband if he was willing to keep her as his wife, although this might, at times, involve her in delicate issues of conscience—if, for example, he insisted on her joining him in social activities which involved some degree of pagan worship.

Similarly, the social ties binding friends and neighbours together were not to be severed. A Christian might with a good conscience accept an invitation to a meal in a pagan home. He should no more ask awkward questions about the history of the food served at the meal than his wife should ask about the joint she bought in the meat market. Perhaps it came from an animal which had been sacrificed to a pagan divinity. What of it? It was neither better nor worse for that; it was in fact sanctified by the word of thanksgiving which the Christian pronounced over it. Normally the question of eating the flesh of animals which had been sacrificed to pagan divinities would arise only for more affluent Christians; the poorer ones would eat meat very seldom.

But there were some activities in which a Christian could hardly engage without compromising his confession—those, for instance, which involved at least a token participation in pagan worship or the countenancing of sexual immorality. Thus an invitation to a banquet in a pagan temple was on a different footing from an invitation to a meal in a private house; whatever took place in a temple took place nominally at least under the patronage of the divinity worshipped there, and could be highly uncongenial to those who now served the living and true God. Here certainly was a situation in which the cross constituted a barrier between the believer and the world.

Christians who refused to take part any longer in such social occasions might well become unpopular with their old companions, even when those occasions did not involved what one New Testament writer calls "wild profligacy" (1 Peter 4:4). So many trade guilds and professional associations were under the nominal patronage of pagan divinities that a Christian could not easily continue membership in them. How, for example, would a silversmith in Ephesus fare if he were converted under Paul's preaching? Could he remain happily in a guild which derived most of its profit from the temple and cult of the great goddess Artemis?

The charges of anti-social sentiment brought against Christians on these grounds made it all the more necessary for them to show that they were not enemies of society in any political sense. It was easy for those who did not like them to lump them along with subversive agitators. Any one who investigated the origins of Christianity could readily discover that Jesus, whom Christians acknowledged as their Lord, had been executed for sedition by sentence of a Roman judge. Therefore strict obedience to the ruling powers is enjoined by Paul and others on Gentile Christians, with the scrupulous paying of taxes and the recognition of the magistrates' authority in all the spheres of life in which it could properly be exercised.

But disputes within the Christian community should be settled within that community; they should not be brought for adjudication before pagan judges. Each Christian church was in some respects like a city within a city, a state within the state, and very much a welfare state. It was the responsibility of well-to-do members to make provision for those in material need. The same principle operated not only within each church, but among churches. Paul is sometimes credited with organizing Gentile Christianity, if not with being the effective founder of the church catholic, but in truth the only enterprise that he is known to have organized was the relief fund for the Jerusalem church which he launched in the churches which he himself planted.

It was a common enterprise like this, rather than any formal organization, that first bound the churches together and gave them a sense of unity, or at least enabled them to express their sense of unity. The basic sense of unity was there already. When Christians visited another city in which a church had been planted, they knew they would find likeminded people, sharing a common faith, a common hope and a common life; this meant, on the most practical level, that they could be sure of congenial hospitality.

This positive bond of union gave cohesion to the Christian groups and to the Christian society as a whole. The negative features, the things they notoriously refrained from doing, were corollaries of this. Each city church or house-church was a social unit, a *collegium* in the eyes of Roman law, with common meals and common acts of worship and a common spirit of love and "belongingness". Exclusion from this common life was the ultimate sanction, but it was invoked only in extreme cases, where a member persisted in behaviour which not only contravened the ethical standards of the believing community but brought it into public disrepute. Exclusion was a matter of the utmost seriousness, for if the community belonged peculiarly to the Lord and was under his protection, the world outside lay under the dominion of evil; to exclude a member from the community was therefore, in effect, to deliver such a person to Satan (1 Corinthians 5:5). Happily, there was hope of recovery for excluded members; the shock of exclusion might indeed bring them to their senses and thus lead to their ultimate salvation.

Membership in those churches was not confined to one social class. Primitive Christianity was not a mass movement of slaves and other depressed groups. If the household codes incorporated in several New Testament letters include directions for Christian slaves (and very unrevolutionary directions at that), they also include directions for Christian slave-owners. The Corinthian Christians are reminded by Paul that they include "not many" who could be called wise, powerful or of noble birth "according to worldly standards" (1 Corinthians 1:26). There would have been no point in using such language to a community drawn from the submerged tenth of society; Paul speaks to them like this in an attempt to deflate their self-esteem. One of their number, Erastus, rose to high municipal office; another, Gaius, had a house large enough to accommodate "the whole church" (Romans 16:23). When someone like Gaius acted as host to the church, the church would probably include his household (his *familia*, to use the Latin term), not only relatives but retainers and slaves; it would span a great part of the social spectrum. Crispus, former ruler of the synagogue, who was one of Paul's first converts in Corinth (1 Corinthians 1:14; Acts 18:8), would also have been well-to-do; rulers of the synagogue were drawn from men and women of substance in the local Jewish community.

Lydia, Paul's first convert in Philippi, was an independent business woman with a house and household of her own (Acts 16:14, 15). Leading women, or wives of leading men, figure conspicuously among the foundation members of the churches of Thessalonica and Beroea (Acts 17:4, 12); the women of Macedonia traditionally enjoyed greater independence than their sisters in the Greek cities farther south.

Those Christians of the first century were not able to cast off completely the social attitudes with which they had grown up, but they were probably able to do so much more thoroughly than western Christians of the twentieth century generally do, because the gospel of Christ crucified, which bound them together, not only formed a barrier between them and the world but dictated a revaluation, and often a reversal, of their previous social values.

People who have been so effectively "desocialized" and "resocialized" are exposed to the risk of developing a sect-mentality, of looking on their group as "a garden walled around", insulated from the encroachments of the wilderness outside. The course of Christian history in those early generations shows that this was not the dominant mentality among the churches. They were encouraged to be outward-looking in their practical charity as well as in their spoken witness. The Thessalonian Christians are urged to "abound in love to one another and to all", to "do good to one another and to all" (1 Thessalonians 3:12; 5:15). The garden was to take over more and more of the wilderness; the world must be rescued from the usurping tyranny of the evil one and brought into joyful allegiance to its true Lord. If Paul speaks of the cross as fencing off the believer from the world, he also views the world as the beneficiary of the redemption accomplished on the cross: "God was in Christ reconciling the world to himself" (2 Corinthians 5:19). The church could not have expanded as it did were it not that so many of its members took the initiative, by word and by action, in being messengers of God's reconciling mercy to their fellow men and women.

Understanding Paul

One of the New Testament writers admitted that in the letters of "our beloved brother Paul" there were "some things . . . hard to understand" (2 Peter 3:15f.). We need not be too surprised, therefore, if we too sometimes find a little difficulty in following his arguments. Yet he expected his readers to understand what he wrote to them, and they were not communities of supermen.

We are at a disadvantage as compared with the first readers of these letters because they were perfectly acquainted with the background of the letters, and we are not. It has often been suggested that in reading Paul's letters today we are like people listening to one end of a telephone conversation. We find it difficult to grasp the meaning of some of the things we hear because we cannot hear what is being said at the other end. A good part of Paul's first letter to the Corinthians consists of a reply to a succession of questions which had been put to Paul in a letter recently sent to him by the Corinthian Christians. Their letter to Paul has not been preserved; we can only infer its contents from the terms in which Paul answers it. Perhaps we could grasp certain points in 1 Corinthians better if we could see the letter to which they refer. And in general the whole situation with which Paul's letters deal, the persons to whom he refers, the incidents which he briefly recalls—all these were matters of common knowledge to his readers, and the merest allusion was enough to show them what Paul had in mind. But we have to do our best to reconstruct the situation, and it is always possible that we may be mistaken because we have lost an important element in it. It has been strongly argued, as we shall see, that 2 Corinthians was not originally a single letter in the form in which we have it now—that it consists of pieces of two or more separate letters written by Paul to his friends at Corinth. In Philippians too, it has been thought, there are signs that two originally separate letters have been joined together. Probably we shall never be able to settle such problems conclusively, simply because we do not know all the relevant details of Paul's relationship with the Corinthian and Philippian churches.

Again, Paul's style is not always easy to follow. This is partly on account of his habit of dictating his letters to an assistant. At times the impetuous torrent of Paul's thought seems to rush forward so swiftly that it outstrips the flow of his words, and his words have to leap over a gap now and then to catch up with his thought. We can only surmise how the assistant contrived to keep up with his words. Time and again Paul starts a sentence that never reaches a grammatical end, for before he is well launched on it a new thought strikes him and he turns aside to digress. Then, when he comes back to the main line, the original opening of the sentence has been forgotten. All this means that Paul is not the smoothest of authors, or the easiest to follow, but it does give us an unmistakable impression of the man himself. Here is a man with something to say, and there is nothing artificial or merely conventional about the way he says it. And what he has to say is so important—for readers of the twentieth century as well as for the first-century Christians in Thessalonica, Corinth and Philippi—that the effort to understand him is abundantly rewarding.

Paul's letters and Christian beginnings

The fact that our New Testament begins with the four gospels and Acts, and then presents us with Paul's letters, tends to obscure for us the original order in which these documents were written. Most of Paul's letters were written before even the earliest of the gospels. The two letters to the Thessalonians are (with the possible exception of the letter to the Galatians) the oldest of the New Testament documents. This means that when Paul refers to the life, death and resurrection of Jesus, or to some of his teaching, he is giving us our earliest surviving evidence. For example, in 1 Corinthians 11:23–26 he tells us how Jesus instituted the Holy Communion and what he said as he did so. The first three gospel-writers also give us a record of this, but Paul's record is older by several years than the earliest of theirs, and must be treated with corresponding respect. We have to think not only of the date when this record was written down in this letter. Paul is not telling the Corinthians something they did not know before; he is reminding them of what he "delivered" to them by word of mouth when he was with them five years earlier. Not only so: what he then "delivered" to them was what he himself had "received" at the beginning of his Christian career, perhaps seventeen years earlier still, and the ultimate authority for the record was derived from the Lord, who instituted the sacrament and spoke the words that explained his action.

There were no written gospels when Paul wrote these letters. Yet the letters were written to Christians —that is to say to people who had heard and believed the gospel story. But they knew it in an oral form, not in written records. Since they knew it, however, it was not necessary for Paul to relate it in his letters to them, except when, for purposes of his own, he thinks it wise to remind them of the gospel which they had heard from his lips. He does this, for example, at the beginning of 1 Corinthians 15, when he wishes to show his Corinthian readers how the resurrection hope is vitally bound up with the saving message which they have already received. But for the most part he regards that message as a foundation which has been well and truly laid, and he goes on to build upon it—to draw out and apply the implications of the gospel for Christian thought and life.

It is only rarely that Paul expressly quotes the teaching of Jesus when he urges on his converts the implications of the gospel. Sometimes, indeed, he does so; in 1 Corinthians, for example, he refers explicitly to Jesus' words about divorce (7:10f.), about the right of gospel preachers to have their material needs supplied (9:14), and about the significance of the

Lord's Supper (11:24f.); and in 1 Thessalonians he
appeals to "the word of the Lord" as his authority for
saying that believers who have died will rise at the
Second Coming of Christ (4:15). But, although such
passages are rare, it is not difficult to discover that
Paul's ethical teaching is based firmly on that of Jesus,
on what he calls "the law of Christ" in 1 Corinthians
9:21.

Paul's converts did not have a written record of the
teaching of Jesus which could be put into their hands
when they believed the gospel. It was very necessary
that they should learn as soon as possible the elements
of the Christian way of life, but they had to depend on
oral teaching for this—teaching given them by Paul
himself or by other Christian instructors, reinforced by
their personal example (to which Paul in particular
repeatedly drew his converts' attention).

At a very early time it appears that a recognized
body of such oral teaching took shape. When Paul
commends the Corinthian Christians for maintaining
"the traditions" (1 Corinthians 11:2), or when he
urges the Thessalonian Christians to "hold to the traditions which you were taught by us, either by word of
mouth or by letter" (2 Thessalonians 2:15), he is
probably referring to this body of teaching. It was so
well known that those who flouted it could be repri-
manded for not living "in accord with the tradition
that you received from us" (2 Thessalonians 3:6). And
this tradition is something that derives its authority
from the teaching and example of Jesus himself; it was
entrusted by him to his apostles to be handed on by

them to their converts and disciples, and so on to succeeding generations.

With the gradual appearance of the New Testament documents, this tradition, which at first existed exclusively in oral form, came to be increasingly enshrined in writing. This must be remembered when we read Paul's letters; he writes with authority, but the authority he claims does not reside in himself personally, but in the Lord whose accredited apostle he is and whose commands he conveys to his converts.

Acts and the Pauline letters

One specially valuable aid to the understanding of Paul's letters, particularly his earlier ones, is provided by his friend and fellow-traveller Luke in *The Acts of the Apostles*. Luke gives us a record of how Paul planted many of the churches to which he later sent letters, and this record is a very helpful background for the study of these letters. For example, in Acts 16 we have an account of the planting of the church at Philippi, in Acts 17:1–10 we have an account of the planting of the church at Thessalonica, and in Acts 18 an account of the planting of the church at Corinth. In introducing the plan of Paul's correspondence with these churches we shall make full use of the information provided by these accounts in Acts.

2
A Word of Hope:
1 Thessalonians

THE PLAN OF 1 THESSALONIANS

The city of Thessalonica

THESSALONICA is an ancient city of Macedonia, also known to-day by its shorter name Salonica. In earlier days it was known as Therme, from the hot springs in its neighbourhood, but it was refounded in 315 B.C. by Cassander, king of Macedonia, and given the name Thessalonica after his wife who was a half-sister of Alexander the Great. When the Romans established their dominance in that area, and made Macedonia a Roman province, Thessalonica became the capital of the province, and that was its status in New Testament times. The city was free to administer its own municipal affairs; this municipal administration was in the hands of a board of five or six chief magistrates known as politarchs (the technical title of the chief magistrates of several Macedonian cities).

The church of Thessalonica

Christianity was first brought to Thessalonica in A.D. 50. Early in that year the apostle Paul had sailed across the Aegean Sea from Asia Minor and landed on its European shore, accompanied by three colleagues. After visiting Philippi, another leading city of Macedonia, and planting a Christian church there, Paul continued his journey westward along the Egnatian Road until he came to Thessalonica. He had left one of his companions, Luke, behind in Philippi; the other two, Silvanus (Silas) and Timothy, accompanied him to Thessalonica.

In Thessalonica they visited the local Jewish synagogue on three successive Sabbath days, and as the Old Testament lessons were read Paul endeavoured to show from them that the Messiah whom they foretold was destined to suffer death and rise again from the dead, and that Jesus, who had within recent years died and risen again, was therefore the expected Messiah. Some of his hearers believed him. Among these there were not only Jews but a considerable number of "God-fearers", that is to say, Gentiles who were loosely attached to the Jewish worship and way of life. It was such God-fearing Gentiles that formed the nucleus of the Christian church in city after city which Paul and his companions visited in the course of their missionary campaigns.

After three Sabbath days the synagogue authorities decided that Paul could no longer be permitted to use their building for what they regarded as subversive propaganda. Paul accordingly detached his converts from the synagogue and formed them into a separate community, the church of Thessalonica. He remained with them for some time, giving them such basic teaching as a young church required. But before he was able to complete this elementary course of teaching, a troublesome situation arose which compelled him to leave the city.

Information was laid before the politarchs that Paul and his colleagues were Jewish messianic agitators, such as had stirred up a great deal of disturbance elsewhere in the Roman Empire, and in particular that they were proclaiming Jesus as emperor in rivalry to the emperor who held sway in Rome. At the same time Paul's Jewish opponents tried to create public disquiet by employing some of the city corner-boys to foment a riotous demonstration against Paul and all his works. Their hope was by such means to alarm the magistrates and make them take hasty and violent action against Paul. The rioters were unable to lay hands on Paul himself, but they seized his host, Jason by name, and some of his other friends in Thessalonica, and dragged them before the magistrates, complaining that these men had harboured plotters of sedition against the emperor.

In the midst of all this excitement it says much for the magistrates that they kept their heads and did not allow themselves to be panicked. They chose what must have seemed to them to be the most effective course in the circumstances; they bound Jason and his companions over to guarantee Paul's good behaviour, which in effect meant his quiet and immediate departure from Thessalonica. They could hardly have done less, for the charge of sedition and the proclamation of a rival emperor was one which would be regarded with the utmost seriousness by the Roman authorities. They might, of course, have given Paul an opportunity to reply in person to the charges brought against him; in that case he would undoubtedly have welcomed the opportunity to show their baselessness and to explain the true nature of the kingship of Christ which the gospel announced. But that would not necessarily have allayed the riotous behaviour of the city mob; and this was what the politarchs considered to be their most urgent task.

Occasion of the letter

Paul, then, found himself in a position where he had no choice but to leave Thessalonica. His friends had guaranteed that he would go away quietly, and he could not let them down. But he went very reluctantly. He had not given his converts all the teaching which he felt was necessary to establish them securely in their new-found faith. He was leaving them to face a good deal of scoffing and petty persecution, if not indeed hostility of a more open and violent kind. They might well think that he had run away from the trouble which his coming had created, and left them in the lurch. He could not rest for thinking of them.

From Thessalonica he went with Silvanus to Beroea, a city of Thessaly, and from there he was taken, for his own safety, to Athens. While he was in Athens he sent Timothy back to Thessalonica to see how his friends and converts were getting on. He himself went on from Athens to Corinth, and waited impatiently for Timothy's return. When Timothy did rejoin him, the news he brought filled Paul with joy and relief. The young church in Thessalonica was standing firm; indeed, it was not only maintaining its faith but propagating it. Paul and his two colleagues, Silvanus and Timothy, wrote at once to congratulate their Thessalonian friends on their steadfastness, and to encourage them to go on as they had begun. In addition they dealt with some of their problems about which Timothy had brought back word. The letter which they wrote is the one which we know as the first letter to the Thessalonians.

Outline of 1 Thessalonians

1. Salutation (1:1)
2. Thanksgiving for their faith and steadfastness (1:2–10)
3. Explanation of the missionaries' conduct (2:1–16)
4. Narrative of events since they left Thessalonica (2:17 – 3:10)
5. Prayer for an early reunion (3:11–13)
6. Encouragement to holy living and brotherly love (4:1–12)
7. Concerning the Second Advent (4:13 – 5:11)
8. General exhortations (5:12–22)
9. Prayer, final greeting and benedictions (5:23–28)

EXPOSITION OF I THESSALONIANS

1. *Salutation* (1:1)

Paul associates his companions and fellow-missionaries, Silvanus (Silas) and Timothy, in the salutation at the beginning of both letters to the church at Thessalonica. Throughout the two letters, where the plural pronoun "we" ("us", "our") is used, all three writers, and especially Paul and Silvanus, take responsibility for what is said. Where Paul is personally responsible, he uses the pronoun "I" (see 1 Thessalonians 2:18; 3:5; 5:27; 2 Thessalonians 2:5; 3:17).

2. *Thanksgiving for their faith and steadfastness* (1:2–10)

After the salutation, Paul and the others launch out into a thanksgiving to God for the good news that has just reached them about their Thessalonian friends. Although Paul and Silvanus had been forced to leave them so abruptly, although they had to put up with much scorn and persecution because of their new allegiance to Christ, their faith did not waver. They rejoiced in everything that they had to endure for the gospel's sake, and far from trying to keep the gospel to themselves, they were so full of it that they had to let everybody know about it.

Their witness was spreading through the whole province of Macedonia, and even farther afield; in the more southerly province of Achaia (Greece), where Paul now was, with his two colleagues, echoes of the Thessalonian Christians' proclamation of their faith were being heard. The missionaries had no need to tell people in Corinth about the faith of the Thessalonians; the news was being blazed abroad almost spontaneously. "Have you heard what happened when Paul and his companions visited Thessalonica?" people were saying. "Have you heard what a welcome they received, what a fine band of converts they made?" And the readers are reminded what actually happened when they heard the Christian message: they gave up their former idolatry, and began to worship the true and living God revealed in the gospel. They heard of Jesus Christ, the Son of God, whom God had raised from the dead, and they began to look forward eagerly to his expected return from heaven as his people's deliverer from the outpouring of divine wrath and judgment which would mark the last day. It is evident from this reference to the preaching at Thessalonica that it had given a large place to the Second Coming of Christ as judge of the living and the dead.

3. *Explanation of the missionaries' conduct* (2:1–16)

Paul's sudden departure from Thessalonica had clearly been the subject of unfavourable comment. "A fine lot these apostles are!" said his detractors. "They come here and gather a crowd of gullible followers; then, when they have made the place too hot for themselves, off they go and leave their dupes to pay for the trouble their visit has stirred up!" Such misrepresentations had to be answered. Paul appeals to his readers' recollection of his behaviour while he was with them as a proof that he and his colleagues had not made any attempt to exploit them or live at their expense. So many wandering charlatans were going about the Roman world in those days, peddling their religious or philosophic wares, that Paul finds it necessary to emphasize the purity of his motives and conduct as contrasted with theirs.

He and his companions had worked day and night to earn their own living while they were engaged in preaching the good news and building up the newly-founded church of Thessalonica. They had a right to claim material support from the people for whose spiritual welfare they were caring, but they chose to forgo this right. They were gentle (verse 7) and not oppressive to their converts. In this way they showed them a good example and commended by their lives the gospel which they proclaimed. Their desire was that their Thessalonian converts should "lead a life worthy of God" (verse 12). In the New Testament, as in the Old, the people of God are expected to display the character of God. God has called these Thessalonians "into his own kingdom and glory" (verse 12). By faith they had already entered into the kingdom of God, but the revelation of its full glory belonged to a day which still lay in the future; they were, however, heirs of that glory and should conduct themselves in a manner befitting that heritage.

In fact, the Thessalonian converts had proved themselves worthy disciples of their teachers. They had their fair share of persecution to face when Paul and Silvanus had to leave them so abruptly, but they did not allow themselves to be discouraged. They endured their persecution in the same spirit as the Palestinian churches had shown when they were persecuted by their Jewish neighbours. The bitterness of the reference to the Jews in verses 14–16 is unparalleled in Paul's extant correspondence, and has been suspected of being an interpolation. It is certainly surprising to find a common anti-Jewish slander among contemporary pagans ("the Jews", they said, "are in opposition to all mankind") reproduced here. On the other hand, it was Jewish agitation that had made the writers leave Thessalonica so abruptly; since then Paul and Silvanus had further experience of Jewish obstruction in Beroea, and the same process was even now being repeated in Corinth. Convinced as they were that their apostolic ministry was fulfilling the purpose of God, they could not but regard their Jewish opponents as endeavouring to thwart the purpose of God, and therefore as incurring the full weight of divine retribution.

4. *Narrative of events since they left Thessalonica* (2:17–3:10)

Since his compulsory departure from Thessalonica Paul had made more than one attempt to return, but these attempts were frustrated. In this he saw evidence of the activity of Satan, the supernatural enemy of truth. It has been suggested that he detected this subtle agency behind the politarchs' decision to make Jason and others guarantors for his own withdrawal from the city. "I Paul", he says (2:18), because, of the other signatories of this letter, Timothy had returned to Thessalonica and Silvanus had paid a brief visit to Macedonia (Acts 18:5), though apparently not to Thessalonica itself. It was hard for him to bear this enforced absence from his converts, because they had become very dear to his heart; they were, moreover, the ground of his hope that he would be able to give a good account of his stewardship at the coming of Christ. If Christ asked him on that day how he had fulfilled his apostolic commission, he would be able to point with pride to such converts as these, as the worthy fruit of his labours. The word "coming" (2:19) is in the original *parousia*, a Greek term used of the arrival of some distinguished personage to pay an official visit. It is used of the Second Advent of Christ 18 times in the New Testament, including seven times in the Thessalonian letters.

In his impatience to make some contact with them, therefore, he sent Timothy back to Thessalonica to encourage them and bring back news of their progress. He could well believe that they were being persecuted for their faith, but they had been warned in advance that this would be their lot. Indeed, it is taken for granted in the New Testament that persecution is a normal experience for Christians. The missionaries could not help wondering, however, whether the persecution might not have proved too much for their Thessalonian friends. Such a thing was almost too terrible to contemplate: if they gave up their new-found faith, all their care and toil for them would appear to have been expended in vain. But great as was their anxiety on their behalf, greater still was their relief

48

when Timothy came back to report that all was well—
that the converts' faith remained unshaken. They could
breathe freely again: "now we live, if you stand fast in
the Lord" (3:8). Now in their joy they pour out their
hearts in thankfulness to God for their converts' steadfastness, and redouble their prayers that the day may
not be far distant when they can go in person to see
them and confirm the faith of the Christians.

5. *Prayer for an early reunion* (3:11–14)

While they pray for this, they pray also that their
converts' love may go on increasing, both for their
fellow Christians and for the wider world outside. In
this important matter of Christian love they already
had an example in the attitude of the missionaries
themselves, who were willing to undergo all sorts of
discomfort and danger for the sake of bringing the
gospel to their fellow men and helping their converts.
Thus they would increase in holiness—for love and
holiness are inseparable in the Christian life—until the
day when they were to stand in God's presence, the day
of Christ's return. The Second Coming of Christ is
mentioned very frequently in the Thessalonian correspondence, but it is mentioned chiefly so that it may be
an incentive to Christians to live and work in a manner
worthy of Christ.

The wording of verse 11, "may our God and Father
himself, and our Lord Jesus, direct our way to you", is
an example of the unforced and natural way in which
those early Christians associated Christ with God in

49

their thinking and speaking. The "saints" or "holy ones" with whom Christ is to come at his Second Advent (verse 13) are probably his attendant angels, to judge by earlier scriptures: angels were regularly in attendance at manifestations of the glory of God (compare Deuteronomy 33:2; Daniel 7:10; Zechariah 14:5; Mark 8:38, etc.).

6. *Encouragement to holy living and brotherly love* (4:1–12)

The writers develop their exhortation to lives of purity and holiness, more particularly with reference to relations between the sexes. Perhaps there was no sphere of life where there was a greater divergence between Christian and pagan ethics than this. They had already received some instruction about this from Paul and his companions, and that instruction had been enforced by the personal example of the missionaries; but further insistence on sexual purity is judged advisable (possibly because Timothy's report had indicated that there was some necessity for it). The Revised Standard Version rendering of verse 4, "that each one of you know how to take a wife for himself", is probably wrong. A more literal rendering is that of the Authorized Version, "that every one of you should know how to possess his vessel", and the phrase "possess his vessel" simply means "control his own body", as the New International Version has it. Only thus could they rise above the pagan standards of sexual morality which surrounded them and lead lives worthy of their Christian confession. Licence in this sphere of life was a breach of the law of love to one's neighbour; and when the writers urge "that no man transgress, and wrong his brother in this matter" (verse 6), they evidently envisage an offence of this kind against a female member of the household of a fellow Christian. But such licence is also an offence against God, who has called his people to lives of holiness and has given them the Holy Spirit to enable them to fulfil this purpose. Unholiness and uncleanness will incur his wrath.

More generally, the readers are urged to practise brotherly love in all the ways of life. They had made a good beginning in this regard; let them persevere. Brotherly love demanded sober and industrious habits: a Christian should not be a busybody, but should be diligent in his daily work so as to "command the respect of outsiders, and be dependent on nobody" (verse 12). Paul himself had taught them this lesson by precept and practice. Christian teaching about holiness and brotherly love is nothing if not practical.

7. *Concerning the Second Advent* (4:13–5:11)

Paul had given his Thessalonian converts some instruction about the Second Advent while he was with them, but he was unable to stay and complete that instruction. They were left with several questions unanswered. It appears that many of them thought that they would all be alive when this event took place. But some of their number died—possibly because of the persecution which they had to bear—and their friends wondered anxiously if this meant that they would forfeit all share in the blessings which believers would enter into at the return of Christ. Timothy on his return probably told Paul and Silvanus about this, and they now write to set the Thessalonians' minds at ease, basing their assurance on an utterance of Christ. Christians who have died, they say, will be at no disadvantage when Christ returns, for the first thing that will happen when he does return will be that "the dead in Christ" will be raised; not until that happens will the believers who are still alive join them to greet their Lord, and be eternally in his presence. The "clouds" of verse 17 symbolize the divine presence, and together with the cry of command and the trumpet call (verse 16) had long since formed part of the verbal imagery denoting the arrival of the day of the Lord (compare Daniel 7:13; Joel 3:16; Matthew 24:30, 31). "God will bring with him" (verse 14) means that God will raise dead believers from the grave, just as he raised Jesus. So death with Christ is but the prelude to resurrection with him.

If any question was raised about the time when this event would take place, the only answer was that it would take by surprise those who were morally unprepared for it. Jesus himself had said: "Take heed, watch; for you do not know when the time will come" (Mark 13:33). But Christians, as the "sons of light" (5:5), would keep alert and be ready for the day whenever it might come. For them the day would mean not wrath but final deliverance (cf. 1:10); whether they were alive or dead when it dawned they would live forever with him who died for them (5:10). Here was ample ground for mutual comfort and encouragement! (4:18; 5:11).

8. *General exhortations* (5:12–22)

Part of Christian discipline consists in obedience to spiritual leaders (5:12, 13). The exhortation of verse 14 seems to be intended more particularly for such leaders; it would be their province primarily to speak sharply to idlers and spongers, and to give support and encouragement where necessary. For the rest, the believers should live in peace with one another, help one another, and show one another the forgiving love of Christ. A spirit of joy, coupled with constant prayer and gratitude to God, should characterize their lives. The injunctions of verses 19–21 refer to the exercise of prophecy, under the impulse of the Holy Spirit, a gift much in evidence in the apostolic church. It was easily counterfeited and called for discriminating judgment, but it was not to be despised, and its genuine exercise was not to be repressed. In general, let them adhere to good and avoid evil in every form.

9. *Prayer, final greeting and benediction* (5:23–28)

Then comes a prayer that God, who has called them to holiness, may make them holy until at last, on the resurrection day, they stand perfect before him. Paul's solemn injunction of verse 27 suggests his determination that every member of the church, including the idlers of verse 14, should hear what he and his colleagues have to say.

3
A Word about the Future:
2 Thessalonians

THE PLAN OF 2 THESSALONIANS

Fresh news from Thessalonica

NOT LONG after they sent their first letter to the Thessalonian church, Paul and his companions received further news which indicated that there were still some problems to be cleared up. They suspected that some of these problems might be due to the arrival in Thessalonica of a forged letter purporting to come from them. Quite plainly some of their teaching about the Second Advent had been misunderstood, so that a number of their friends there imagined that its coming lay in the immediate future, while a few even considered that, seeing the end of all things was so imminent, there was no point in going on working. They cleared up the misunderstanding by pointing out that certain events had to take place before the Second Advent could be expected, and they addressed some sharp words to those who would not work and thus became a charge upon the charity of their fellow Christians. It is evident that, for whatever reason, an unhealthy degree of end-of-the-world excitement had been stirred up in Thessalonica, and this second letter was intended to serve as a sobering corrective to the excitement.

Relation to 1 Thessalonians

A close examination of the relation between the two letters to the Thessalonians raises a number of complicated problems, to which various solutions have been offered. One suggestion, for example, is that the two letters were originally written in the reverse sequence to that in which they have been transmitted to us; that 2 Thessalonians was actually written first, and that when Paul sent Timothy from Athens to Thessalonica to see how the Christians were faring there, he gave him this letter to deliver to them. But if this solution appears to solve some of the problems, it raises new ones. On the whole, the account given above seems the most satisfactory.

Outline of 2 Thessalonians

1. Salutation (1:1–2)
2. Thanksgiving and encouragement (1:3–12)
3. Events which must precede the day of the Lord (2:1–12)
4. Further thanksgiving and encouragement (2:13 – 3:5)

5. The need for discipline (3:6–15)
6. Prayer, final greeting and benediction (3:16–18)

EXPOSITION OF 2 THESSALONIANS

1. *Salutation (1:1–2)*

The language used rules out the suggestion sometimes made that the two letters were sent to different
sections of the Thessalonian church.

2. *Thanksgiving and encouragement (1:3–12)*

The Thessalonian Christians might have protested
that the writers' commendation of them in the previous
letter was excessive: "No", they say, "we are bound to
give thanks to God always for you" (verse 3). Their
persecution showed no sign of abating; but they are
asked to look on this as something which attests their
fitness for the heavenly kingdom, and something, too,
which ensures the righteous judgment of God on their
enemies at the return of Christ. For Christians, however, that day will bring glory; in fact, Christ will be
glorified in them when they are glorified with him.
But Paul and his colleagues pray that here and now the
Thessalonian Christians may be worthy of this wonderful destiny which lies before them, so that Christ
may be glorified in them at the present time. The
"flaming fire" of verse 7 and its accompaniments are
frequent features of the manifestation of God's presence
and power in the Old Testament (compare Deuteronomy 33:2; Psalm 50:3; Daniel 7:9, 10, etc.).

3. *Events which must precede the day of the Lord* (2:1–12)

Evidently the previous letter had not succeeded in clearing up all the Thessalonians' difficulties about the Second Coming. Some of them had the impression that this "day of the Lord" was imminent, if indeed it had not already set in, and that therefore there was no point in carrying on with their ordinary duties. They are now assured that this is not so, and that they are not to believe it, even if it is announced by a "prophet" in church or conveyed to them as a message, orally or in writing, from Paul himself.

Certain things must precede the day of the Lord, and these things had not yet taken place. For these things to take place, the restraint on the forces of lawlessness and anarchy at present exercised by the power of law and order must be removed, so that lawlessness would manifest itself in all its evil activity. There would be a world-wide rebellion against God, the source of all true law and order, and this spirit of rebellion would be incarnated in a sinister personage called "the man of lawlessness" or "the lawless one". During his heyday he would claim divine honours, and so skilfully would he hoodwink men and women by impressive signs, performed by Satan's aid, that they would acknowledge his claims and follow him blindly to perdition. (Our own generation has seen examples of the awful truth of Paul's words.) But this person—elsewhere in the New Testament referred to as "Antichrist"—would meet his destined destruction at the glorious appearing of the true Christ.

Since, however, Antichrist had not yet appeared, the day of Christ could not yet be here. Antichrist had not yet appeared because of the influence of a restraining power (verses 6, 7), by which Paul probably indicates the Roman Empire. He does not express himself more explicitly, because a reference to the empire's being taken "out of the way" (verse 7) might seem to give colour to the charge of sedition brought against him while he was at Thessalonica.

He makes it clear that he is not telling his Thessalonian friends all this for the first time (verse 5), but they have not grasped the implication of his former teaching on the subject. His language about the man of lawlessness goes back in principle to the warning of Jesus about "'the abomination of desolation' usurping a place which is not his" (Mark 13:14, New English Bible; note that in Mark's account the abomination of desolation is personal). And indeed, ten years before the writing of this letter, a foreshadowing of Antichrist's claim to divine honours had been seen when the mad Emperor Gaius demanded that his statue should be erected as an object of worship in the Jerusalem temple (compare verse 4). Gaius's madness was frustrated by the forces of law and order, which brought him down; but one day another would succeed where Gaius had failed. So long, however, as imperial order survived in its present form, the "mystery of lawlessness", though already at work beneath the surface, would be prevented from breaking forth in all its malignity and leading the world astray in its revolt against God—a revolt which would be put down by the advent of Christ.

One aspect of the activity of "the mystery of lawlessness", in Paul's mind, would be opposition to the gospel such as was stirred up in Thessalonica, Corinth and elsewhere; and he had good reason to be grateful for the protection which Roman law afforded him against such opposition. But it was urgently necessary to cover as much ground as possible against the time when that protection would be withdrawn, and the hostile forces be free to do their work without restraint.

4. *Further thanksgiving and encouragement* (2:13 − 3:5)

But the Thessalonians need not be alarmed, provided they stand fast in their faith and adhere to the "traditions" which Paul and his friends delivered to them (2:15). These "traditions" comprised the primitive deposit of Christian truth, delivered by Christ to his apostles and by them to their converts. And indeed there was good hope that they would stand firm, in accordance with the purpose and choice of God, who had given them his Spirit that they might be made perfect in holiness, and ultimately share the glory of Christ on the day of his manifestation. So the writers pray for their spiritual progress and establishment (2:16, 17), and ask for their prayers in return—more especially, that the gospel might triumph in Corinth and other places as it had triumphed in Thessalonica (3:1). The "evil men" from whom they seek deliverance (3:2) are primarily those who put obstacles in the way of the gospel's advance. But such deliverance comes ultimately from God, and Paul expresses his confidence in the sufficiency of God's grace for himself and his readers alike.

5. *The need for discipline* (3:6–15)

But however much the writers felt bound to thank God for their converts' faith and perseverance, there were some members of the community who required a stern warning. These were the idlers, who imagined that the Christian hope exempted them from the necessity of earning an honest living. These inevitably became a charge on others and brought the Christian cause into disrepute. They were ignoring the Christian "tradition" and the apostolic example alike by such behaviour. The others, therefore, must give them no countenance, so that they might be shamed into doing the right thing, minding their own business and earning their own living (compare 1 Thessalonians 4:11, 12).

6. *Prayer, final greeting and benediction* (3:16–18)

Thus this second letter to the Thessalonians is brought to an end with a prayer for their peace, by grace of him who is "the Lord of peace". Paul draws their attention to his personal autograph which authenticates all his letters as his. For the most part he dictated his letters, but added some words at the end (sometimes, as here, including his signature) in his own handwriting. Any letter purporting to come from him should be ignored if it did not bear this authentication (compare 2:2). The authentication here implies that he endorsed those parts of the letter for which his companions were primarily responsible.

4
Practical Counsel on Moral Issues: 1 Corinthians

THE PLAN OF I CORINTHIANS

The gospel in Corinth

WHEN PAUL came to Corinth in the autumn of
A.D. 50 he settled down there for eighteen months.
Corinth had been for centuries one of the most important cities of Greece. Situated on the Isthmus of Corinth
it occupied an almost ideal position for commercial
enterprise, at the junction of land routes running
north and south, and at the junction of sea routes to
west and east. It was destroyed by a Roman army in
146 B.C. and lay derelict for a century, until Julius
Caesar rebuilt it and gave it the status of a Roman
colony. Seventeen years later (27 B.C.) Corinth became
the seat of administration of the Roman province of
Achaia—that is to say, the whole of Greece to the
south of Macedonia.

The restored Corinth speedily acquired an unen-
viable reputation which the earlier Corinth had

enjoyed—a reputation for sexual vice which was out-
standing even by the fairly lax standards of Graeco-
Roman paganism. "Behaving like a Corinthian" was a
common way of referring to the more outrageous forms
of wantonness. A city with such a reputation might
have been thought to provide unpromising soil for
planting the Christian seed; but Paul made many
converts in Corinth, and before he left the city there
was a flourishing church there.

As in Thessalonica, Paul made the synagogue his
first base of operations, but when the synagogue
authorities could tolerate him no longer he took his
converts and followers away and found a meeting-place
for them in the house of a Corinthian citizen, Gaius
Titius Justus, who lived next door to the synagogue.
As in Thessalonica, his Jewish opponents tried to stir
up trouble for him and lodged an accusation against
him before Gallio, the Roman proconsul of Achaia.
The charge was that Paul was propagating an illegal
religion. But Gallio decided quickly that, whatever it
was that Paul was propagating, it was from the view-
point of Roman law some variety of the Jewish religion,
which already enjoyed the protection of Roman law.
He therefore refused to take the matter up. The decision
of so important an official as Gallio was bound to be
followed as a precedent by other magistrates, and the
consequence was that Paul was able to carry on his
apostolic work with the protection of Roman law, not
only for the remainder of his stay in Corinth, but for
the next ten years.

Disquieting reports from Corinth

Shortly after Paul left Corinth he settled in Ephesus, on the east shore of the Aegean Sea, and spent the greater part of three years (from autumn of 52 to spring of 55) in the evangelization of the Roman province of Asia. But his Ephesian ministry was punctuated from time to time by disquieting reports of his converts in Corinth. Some of them had not appreciated sufficiently the moral implications of the gospel, and were disposed to slip back into traditional Corinthian behaviour. News of this came to Paul and he sent them a letter in which he warned them "not to associate with anyone who bears the name of brother if he is guilty of immorality or greed, or is an idolater, reviler, drunkard, or robber—not even to eat with such a one" (1 Corinthians 5:9–11).

Not long afterwards, further news was brought to him by members of the household of a Corinthian lady of substance named Chloe. They told him that the church was beginning to split up into cliques, called after the names of various Christian leaders—Paul himself; Peter, leader of the original twelve apostles; Apollos, the learned preacher from Alexandria. Others actually called themselves the party of Christ, as though Christ were a party-leader and not their common Lord. Paul set himself to deal with this situation; he wrote to say that this party spirit was an impoverishment for those who yielded to it, for Christ was Lord of them all, and all of them ought to benefit from the ministry of Paul, Peter, Apollos, and every other servant of Christ.

Paul hoped to pay them a personal visit soon and deal with their problems on the spot; meanwhile, he was sending Timothy to them as his trusted representative—perhaps he had already sent him.

The Corinthians' letter to Paul

He was about to close the letter and give it to a messenger to carry to Corinth when three other members of the Corinthian church arrived in Ephesus with a letter for him, asking several very practical questions. Moreover, the bearers of the letter had some fresh information for him: there was a case of flagrant immorality in the church which actually shocked the pagans of Corinth; a spirit of litigiousness was rife in the church and Christians were prosecuting one another in pagan courts; one party in the church was asserting its freedom from all legal restraint.

Paul therefore went on to dictate much more of the letter which he had almost finished. He deals drastically with those situations which called for drastic treatment, and he answers the questions in the Corinthians' letter one by one. At last the letter was finished and taken to Corinth (by one of his Corinthian visitors, perhaps)—the letter which we know as 1 Corinthians.

Outline of 1 Corinthians

1. Salutation (1:1–9)
2. Paul's judgment on reports brought by the members of Chloe's household:

 (a) Party strife (1:10–4:5)

 (b) Criticism of Paul's apostleship (4:6–21)

3. Paul's judgment on reports brought by Stephanas and his companions:

 (a) A case of flagrant immorality (5:1–13)

 (b) A spirit of litigiousness (6:1–8)

 (c) Interpreting liberty as licence (6:9–20)

4. Paul's reply to the Corinthians' letter:

 (a) The marriage question (7:1–40)

 (b) Eating sacrificial meat: liberty and charity (8:1–11:1)

 (c) Veiling of women at public worship (11:2–16)

 (d) Scandals at the Lord's Supper (11:17–34)

 (e) Spiritual gifts: the supremacy of love (12:1–14:40)

 (f) The resurrection faith (15:1–58)

 (g) The collection for Jerusalem (16:1–4)

5. Personal news (16:5–18)

6. Final greetings (16:19–24)

EXPOSITION OF I CORINTHIANS

1. *Salutation and thanksgiving* (1:1–9)

Those whom Paul addresses form "the church of God which is at Corinth" (verse 2), but they are bound together in one holy fellowship with all those in every place who acknowledge the same Lord as they do. Sosthenes, whom Paul here associates with himself (verse 1), may be a member of their own church, possibly the former ruler of the synagogue who received rough handling from the city mob when the case against Paul was dismissed by Gallio (Acts 18:17). One thing that emerges from these opening words of greeting is that the Christians of Corinth were richly endowed with a variety of spiritual gifts—a subject on which Paul enlarges later in the letter. The reference to their waiting "for the revealing of our Lord Jesus Christ" (verse 7) indicates a similar expectancy to that at Thessalonica (compare 1 Thessalonians 1:10).

2. *Paul's judgment on reports brought by the members of Chloe's household:*

(a) Party strife (1:10–4:5)

Those who called themselves Paul's party probably thought that they were thus honouring their own apostle and founder, as against those who were enrolling themselves under the names of other leaders; but Paul disapproved of the slogan "I belong to Paul" as much as of any of the other party slogans. Apollos of Alexandria had gone to Corinth not long after Paul's departure from it (compare Acts 18:24–28). The people who said "I belong to Apollos" were probably those who were captivated by his learning and eloquence, and his mastery of the Old Testament scriptures which he may have interpreted in the highly allegorical fashion current in his native Alexandria. The existence of a party which claimed to be Peter's need not imply that Peter himself had paid a visit to Corinth, although we cannot be sure that he did not. But we may well envisage a visit to Corinth by Palestinian Christians who belittled Paul's apostleship and pointed out that the only genuine apostles of Christ were those who accompanied him during his ministry, and that Peter was the leader of these. They may even have appealed to some such saying of Jesus as "you are Peter, and on this rock I will build my church" (Matthew 16:18).

It is more difficult to decide about those who said "I belong to Christ". Of course, every Christian could say this, but Paul's indignant question "Is Christ divided?" suggests that the name of Christ was being used in a partisan sense. In that case the people who so used it were perhaps those who went to the limit in asserting their freedom from all conventional restraint—they would thus represent the opposite extreme from Peter's party, who probably insisted on the continuing validity of the law of Israel.

Paul thanks God that he gave no one any pretext for claiming him as a party leader; he had baptized only a handful of the Corinthian Christians, his earliest converts in the city. (The other converts would have been baptized by Paul's colleagues or by one of their fellow Corinthians who had become Christians before them.) Nor had Paul used learned arguments (such as the followers of Apollos doubtless appreciated) but proclaimed the message of the cross of Christ in the plainest terms (1:17).

Many of the Corinthians set much store by secular wisdom and philosophy. But, says Paul, the message of the cross has no standing in the light of secular wisdom and philosophy. Gentiles thought it sheer folly to expect them to accept as a leader and deliverer one who was not wise enough to save himself from such a death as crucifixion, while to Jews the proclamation of a crucified Messiah was self-contradictory, a scandalous blasphemy. Yet those Corinthian Christians had to admit that the message of the cross had done for them something that all the wisdom in the world could not have done: it had brought them salvation; it had proved itself to be the very power and wisdom of God. God's power and wisdom had proved themselves thus to be far superior to secular power and wisdom; why then should Christians assess the gospel, or preachers of the gospel, by the standards of secular power and wisdom? Let them learn to make their boast in God alone, whose wisdom, displayed in Christ, had accomplished their salvation, with all the blessings that accompany salvation (1:18–31).

Paul, it appears, cut an unimpressive figure when he came to Corinth, and his preaching was not garnished with rhetorical graces. Yet it was effective in leading many of his hearers to faith in Christ—and this, he says, was proof that the power behind his preaching was the Holy Spirit's, and not any attractiveness or eloquence of his own (2:1–5).

Yet, elementary as they might think his teaching to be (by contrast, say, with Apollos's), he could impart higher forms of wisdom to those whose spiritual maturity was adequate to take them in. But these forms of wisdom could be learned in no secular schools; they concerned the eternal purpose of God with regard to his people. The supernatural powers controlling the godless world had no inkling of this divine wisdom; otherwise they would not have encompassed the crucifixion of Christ and thus unwittingly ensured their own defeat (2:6–8). The quotation in 2:9 bears a resemblance to Isaiah 64:4 but comes from an unknown source; in the second century A.D. the words were believed to be a saying of Jesus.

But the higher wisdom of which Paul spoke was spiritual truth and could be grasped only by spiritual men, men whose thinking was controlled by the Holy Spirit, the Spirit of wisdom, and not by the prevalent fashions of secular thought. To the "unspiritual" or natural man, the higher wisdom of God was meaningless, if not foolishness, because he lacked the spiritual organs to understand it. But the spiritual man receives the gift of discernment and discrimination; he can appreciate the mind of God because he has been given the mind of Christ (2:10–16).

Were the Corinthian Christians, then, not sufficiently mature to be taught this higher wisdom? No, says Paul. They might pride themselves on their wisdom; they might boast in their rich endowment with spiritual gifts; but their spiritual immaturity was clearly demonstrated by their indulgence in party-spirit. If they had not grasped that Paul and Apollos were but servants of Christ, used by Christ to fulfil his purpose in them, then evidently they had not reached Christian maturity (3:1–4).

Paul and Apollos each did the service assigned to him by Christ. Paul sowed the seed, Apollos came and watered it; but it was God who made it grow. Or, to change the figure, Paul laid the foundation, Apollos laid the upper courses; but the building was God's. There was nothing wrong with the foundation; Christ himself is the one foundation. But others who come along after the foundation is laid should consider carefully what kind of material they are using for the superstructure—and it is not primarily Apollos that Paul has in mind now. Paul had taught his converts the basic truths of the gospel; what sort of teaching were later visitors to Corinth giving them? Was it teaching that would stand the fiery test of persecution? Was it teaching that would stand the searching test of the final judgment? In a fire which broke out suddenly and swept swiftly through one of those ancient cities, the structures of durable material would stand while wooden shacks and the like would go up in smoke. The day of divine testing would be like that, and would reveal the quality of the builders' workmanship. Good workmanship would be rewarded; faulty workmanship would be consumed. The salvation of the workman would not be jeopardized, however, because that depended on God's grace, not on his own workmanship (3:5–15).

Party strife and similar activity desecrated the building of God. They must remember that, as a community of believers in Christ, they were God's temple, inhabited by his Spirit. God would not deal lightly with those who desecrated his holy temple (3:16–17).

Let them then adopt the standards of divine wisdom instead of judging everything by the standards of secular wisdom. And then, instead of using Christian teachers' names as party slogans, they would see that Paul and Apollos and Peter and the others were given by Christ to them all, not just to a few. Servants of Christ, commissioned by him to dispense the mysteries of divine revelation to his people—that is how they should be regarded. And they should be assessed not in terms of their popularity but in terms of their faithfulness to the one who commissioned them. Paul himself therefore is not over-concerned about their estimate of him; the Lord's final estimate is what counts with him. It is premature for anyone to assess a servant of Christ before the day of Christ's decisive assessment. Hidden motives will then be brought to light and each servant will receive the commendation that is his due (3:18 – 4:5).

(b) Criticism of Paul's apostleship (4:6–21)

In his previous arguments Paul has used the names of himself and Apollos by way of example, but he knows very well that neither he nor Apollos was guilty of fostering party spirit. They were colleagues who appreciated each other, and other would-be leaders might well learn from these two to reject any thought of setting one above the other. No teacher can impart anything that he has not first received; why then should he give himself airs as though he owed no debt to any teacher of his own? (4:6–7).

Paul and his fellow apostles had no easy time as they carried out their appointed tasks. They were continually exposed to slander, persecution, destitution, danger and death. But the Corinthian Christians, in their own estimation, had reached the highest stage of Christian attainment. He speaks ironically, but he does not wish to hurt or shame them, but rather to let them see the proper path. Among all their teachers he is the only one who has a father's affection for them, for they are his children in Christ. They will do well to follow the example which he has set them. For the present he is sending Timothy to them, but soon he plans to come himself. Then those of their number who talk so slightingly of him in his absence will have an opportunity of speaking their mind to his face. But he will be able to see whether there is anything more to them than talk. It will, in any case, depend on themselves whether his visit will be a happy and friendly occasion for them all, or whether he will have to deal with them severely (4:8–21).

3. *Paul's judgment on reports brought by Stephanas and his companions:*

(a) A case of flagrant immorality (5:1–13)

At this juncture three other visitors from Corinth came to Ephesus with a letter to Paul from the Corinthian church—Stephanas, Fortunatus and Achaicus (compare 16:17). But in addition to handing over the letter, they told Paul about further developments in the Corinthian church, some of them of a most disturbing nature. So Paul proceeded to dictate more of his letter.

First, there was a scandal in the church which might

well shock even the hardened pagans of Corinth: a man was cohabiting with his father's wife, and some members of the church actually thought that this was a fine assertion of Christian liberty. This was bringing the Christian name into public disrepute, and the severest measures were necessary: the church must meet immediately (and Paul would be with them in spirit) to pass solemn sentence of excommunication on the offender. This was as necessary for his own ultimate salvation as for the well-being and reputation of the church. If behaviour of this kind were tolerated it would corrupt the whole community as surely as a little leaven makes the whole batch of dough ferment. The reference to leaven leads him to use the Jewish festival of unleavened bread, which followed the passover, as an illustration of the purity of life which should mark those for whom Christ had died as the true passover sacrifice (5:1–8).

In a previous letter (now apparently lost) he had told them not to keep company with fornicators; he now makes it clear that he meant that they should not tolerate such people within the Christian brotherhood. Of course in the ordinary business of life one cannot avoid having dealings with people whose morals leave much to be desired; but the Christian fellowship must be kept pure.

(b) A spirit of litigiousness (6:1–8)

Paul's informants had told him that some members of the Corinthian church were prosecuting others in the city law-courts. This action had really shocked the apostle. If fellow Christians cannot agree, why cannot they submit their disputes to the arbitration of members of their own fellowship instead of taking them to pagan judges, men who have no status in the church? (This is probably the proper sense of the words "those who are least esteemed by the church" at the end of verse 4.) It would be more fitting to put up with injustice uncomplainingly than to wash their dirty linen in public and endanger the good name of the church. On a coming day, as had been foretold in Daniel 7:22, 27, the saints, the people of God, would take part with their Lord in the judgment of the world; even angels would then be subject to their judgment. Could it be, then, that at this present time there was no member of their fellowship wise enough to be entrusted with adjudication in the petty matters that they were quarrelling about? They ought to be ashamed of themselves.

(c) Interpreting liberty as licence (6:9–20)

Paul now reverts to the subject of those Corinthian Christians who thought that the gospel emancipated them from the restraints of what they regarded as conventional morality. "All things are lawful for me" seems to have been these people's motto. Very well, says Paul, but all things are not helpful, especially if a man becomes enslaved by them. These people took the ultra-spiritual line that anything that had to do with the body was morally and religiously irrelevant. As for food, well—"Food is meant for the stomach and the stomach for food", they said. The food and the stomach will both disappear; why be over-concerned about them? Because, says Paul, the body belongs to the Lord; it comes within the scope of his redeeming work and will one day be raised from death by his power.

Here and now a Christian should glorify God in his body, for his body is a temple of the Holy Spirit and ought therefore to be kept pure. Even food is not irrelevant in this regard; but food is a subject to which Paul will revert later. For the moment he emphasizes that sex-relations are not morally neutral matters, as some were inclined to argue—no doubt under the influence of the notoriously lax standards of Corinthian behaviour. To indulge in illicit sex-relations, he urges, is to prostitute the members of Christ, to desecrate the temple of the Holy Spirit. Such relations can never be regarded as isolated actions, for they have a profound effect on the personalities of both the parties concerned. Formerly the Corinthian Christians had been as careless as their neighbours in these times, but now they had been cleansed by God and made his holy people; they must therefore live accordingly.

4. *Paul's reply to the Corinthians' letter*

(a) *The marriage question* (7:1–40)

Paul now turns to deal one by one with the questions raised in the letter which members of the Corinthian church had sent him—and first of all came a composite question dealing with all the aspects of marriage. By contrast with the ultra-libertarian party, there were no doubt some in the church who took an extremely ascetic line and expressed the view: "It is well for a man not to touch a woman." I agree, says Paul, but in view of human nature it is quite an impracticable rule to impose. I myself am unmarried, he goes on, and should be glad to see all Christians free from the distractions which marriage brings; but few have the necessary gift from God enabling them to live like this. So, for Christians in general, monogamy is the rule, with a mutual willingness on the part of husband and wife to grant each other the proper rights and privileges of the conjugal state.

Paul's personal view is plain enough, but he does not dream of enforcing it on others. If people ask for his judgment he will give it, but his own judgment does not have the binding force of a commandment of Christ. Where an explicit commandment of Christ is available on any of the points raised, that is an end of controversy; for example, it is on the authority of Christ (compare Mark 10:9–12) that he rules that a Christian wife should not leave her husband and a Christian husband should not divorce his wife (verses 10, 11). If, however, a pagan husband or wife refuses to go on living with a Christian partner, that is different; the Christian partner is no longer bound by the marriage tie in such a case. But if the pagan partner is content to remain, so much the better; he or she may then be won for Christ (verses 12–16).

Some Christians at Corinth, possibly by way of reaction from the surrounding immorality, had undertaken vows of celibacy (verses 25ff.). Were such vows completely binding? Here Paul again shows his sound practical wisdom. He himself found the celibate state congenial, and he knew that in times of persecution a Christian with family responsibilities might find it more difficult to take an absolutely uncompromising stand for the faith than one who was free from such "entanglements". But he knew very well that vows of celibacy might be undertaken rashly, by people who later found it almost impossible to preserve such vows. Very well, let them marry; they have committed no sin. Similarly, an engaged couple might decide to live together in virginity instead of getting married, but might find later that this unnatural companionship was imposing too great a strain on them; or the man might feel that he was treating the woman unfairly in depriving her of the joys to which she could look forward as a wife and mother. In that case, says Paul, "let them marry—it is no sin" (verse 36). But he indicates his own feelings in the matter when he says that "he who marries his betrothed does well; and he who refrains from marriage will do better" (verse 38). Similarly, a widow is free to remarry, provided that she marries within the Christian fellowship; "but in my judgment she is happier if she remains as she is. And I think that I have the Spirit of God" (verse 40).

Throughout this chapter the care with which Paul distinguishes his own judgment (which his readers are free to accept or reject) from the Lord's commandment (which is binding on them all) suggests that Christians in apostolic days were not so ready as is sometimes thought to ascribe to Christ rulings which actually originated in the apostolic church.

(b) Eating sacrificial meat: liberty and charity (8:1–11:1)

The buying of butcher meat in Corinth and other pagan cities presented some Christians with a conscientious problem. Much of the flesh exposed for sale in the market came from animals which had originally been sacrificed to a pagan deity. The pagan deity received his token portion; the rest of the flesh might be sold by the temple authorities to the retail merchants, and many pagan purchasers might be willing to pay a little more for their meat because it had been "consecrated" to some deity. Among the Christians there were some with a robust conscience who knew that the meat was neither better nor worse for its association with the pagan deity, and were quite happy to eat it; others were not so happy about it, and felt that somehow the meat had become "infected" by its idolatrous association. At an earlier date the Council of Jerusalem had instructed Gentile converts to refrain from eating "what has been sacrificed to idols" (Acts 15:29). What did Paul think?

On the one hand, Paul ranged himself with those who knew that there was no substance in the pagan deities, and that a Christian was at perfect liberty to eat meat of this kind. But knowledge was not everything; the claims of love were to be considered. He himself was prepared to forgo his liberty if by insisting on it he would set a harmful example to a fellow Christian with a weaker conscience. If a Christian who thought the eating of idol meat was wrong was encouraged by the example of his robuster brother to eat some, the resultant damage to his conscience would be debited to the other's lack of charity and consideration (8:1–13).

But Paul's reference to his own readiness to forgo his liberty in the interests of others reminds him that some of his critics argued that this very readiness of his was a sign that he was none too sure in his own mind that he was a genuine apostle. There were a number of rights which the Palestinian apostles claimed and exercised; why did not Paul avail himself of these? They allowed themselves to be supported by their converts and others among whom they ministered; Paul preferred to earn his own living. They took their wives round with them on their missionary and pastoral visitations; Paul denied himself the comfort of a wife's company. Surely, it was argued, Paul would avail himself of these privileges if he knew himself to be a properly commissioned apostle.

Paul's reply was this. Elsewhere his apostleship might be questioned, but it could not be questioned in Corinth. The very existence of the Corinthian church was the proof of his apostolic status and ministry; it was God's own seal, set upon his eighteen months' service in that city. His apostleship was committed to his trust by Jesus himself, whom he had seen face to face (that is to say, after his rising from the dead; compare 15:8).

He agreed about the rights and privileges of an apostle. The soldier earns his pay; the labourer deserves his perquisites. The principle is expressed in the Old

Testament law which forbade the muzzling of an ox while it was treading out the corn, because the beast was entitled to some of the corn in return for its work (verse 9, quoting Deuteronomy 25:4). Christ directed his disciples, when he sent them out to preach and heal, to live at the expense of those among whom they ministered (compare Luke 10:7). Paul has a right to be maintained by his converts. If he does not make use of that right, it is because he chooses not to make use of it, lest any should say that he preached the gospel for material gain. There are some things in which he has no choice; preaching the gospel is one of these. This he is under divine compulsion to do. But he is free to choose whether or not to make his preaching free of charge to his hearers, and he exercises this freedom of choice by keeping himself. Paul, by the way, always shows a remarkable sense of delicacy where money matters are concerned (9:1–18).

Paul is a free man, set free by the Lord. But he exercises his freedom by becoming every man's slave, by being "all things to all men" with an apostolic versatility which some lesser spirits dubbed inconsistency. Among the Jews he lived as a Jew, among the Gentiles as a Gentile, in order that he might win both Jews and Gentiles for Christ. The interests of the gospel were paramount; all else was subordinated to this (9:19–23).

For Paul was very conscious that one day he must render an account to the Lord who had sent him forth as his apostle; therefore he disciplined himself, keeping one goal in view, like a serious athlete. There was a prize to be won at the end of the race, but Paul kept in mind the possibility that he himself might be disqualified, after he had taught others how to run (9:24–27).

He then comes back to the subject of idolatrous associations (chapter 10). He uses the Old Testament story of the Israelites' escape from Egypt and journey through the wilderness as an object lesson. The Corinthian Christians too had been baptized, were sustained by spiritual food and refreshed by spiritual drink. When Paul says "the Rock was Christ" (10:4) he means that he is not thinking so much of the material rock from which Moses brought water for the Israelites (Exodus 17:6; Numbers 20:11), but of the divine Rock celebrated in the Song of Moses (Deuteronomy 32:4, etc.), whom Paul identifies with the preincarnate Christ. Yet all the wonderful blessings enjoyed by the Israelites in those bygone days did not save them from judgment and death when they committed idolatry and put God to the test in other ways, and the tale of what happened to them then is recorded so that Christians to-day may be warned by their example, and may be encouraged to look to God for deliverance in temptation's hour (10:6–13).

It is therefore imperative for Christians to have no truck with idol-worship. Christians, by virtue of their sharing in the Holy Communion, are partakers of the blood and body of Christ; can they at the same time, even in appearance, be partakers of false gods? Here Paul is probably thinking of more than buying and eating the meat of animals which were presented to idols. He probably has in view Christians who accept invitations from pagan friends to attend banquets in pagan temples. At such banquets not only was the meat dedicated to a false god; the whole occasion was expressly organized under the patronage of that god. Could a Christian, who sat at the Lord's table, feel equally at home at the table of an idol which, if it represented anything at all, represented a demon? The ultra-libertarians might argue that all things were lawful; but all things were not helpful, nor did all things build up a sound Christian character either in oneself or in those whose lives might be influenced. If, on the other hand, the invitation was to a meal in a private house, the case was different: a Christian was free to go and to eat whatever was set before him without asking questions. But if he saw that his attitude to meat which had been dedicated to idols was being made the test of the genuineness of his Christianity, he would do well to refrain from eating it. The glory of God and the spiritual welfare of others should be a Christian's chief consideration in eating and drinking, or in anything else. In all this they might take Paul for an example, as he in turn endeavoured to follow Christ's example (10:14–11:1).

(c) Veiling of women at public worship (11:2–16)

Some of the women in the Corinthian church were disposed to assert their Christian freedom by innovations in dress—in particular, by discarding the veil which concealed their hair when they took part in the services of the church (possibly after the example of some pagan prophetesses who prophesied with dishevelled hair). But such a breach of convention would seem to lend colour to the charges of immorality which some people were too ready to level against Christian meetings. Paul therefore recommends that women wear a veil when they pray or prophesy in church, and reinforces his words by various arguments, such as the place of woman in the hierarchy of creation (11:10), and the fact that her abundant hair shows that God from the first intended her head to be covered (11:15). In verse 10 Paul calls her head-covering her "authority", meaning that it symbolized her right to pray and prophesy as a responsible member of the congregation. In verses 11 and 12 he stresses the interdependence of men and women, rather than the dependence of one sex on the other.

(d) Scandals at the Lord's Supper (11:17-34)

It was evidently their custom to come together for a communal meal, in the course of which they took the Holy Communion. But the meal had ceased to be truly communal, for those who brought food and drink ate and drank what they brought instead of sharing it round, so that, by the time the Communion was to be taken, the richer members were too full to be in a proper spiritual state for it, while the poorer members were still hungry. This was an outrage upon the sacred occasion; it was impossible for people in that condition truly to partake of the Lord's Supper (11:20).

Paul goes on to remind them how Jesus instituted the Supper on the night of his betrayal (11:23-25);

this "tradition", which he had already delivered to them, stemmed, like all true Christian tradition, from the Lord himself (compare verse 2). It should be realized that what Paul gives us here is the oldest account of the institution of the Holy Communion that we have, up to ten years older than the account given in our earliest Gospel. He reminds the Corinthians of the story of the institution in order that they may see how completely their unseemly behaviour frustrates the purpose for which the holy supper was ordained by Christ. It is a most serious desecration of Christ's ordinance to act as they are doing; no wonder that sickness and untimely death are rife among them (verse 30). Let them take the Supper in a proper condition of body and soul, and thus avoid the judgment which waits for those who eat in an unworthy and unbrotherly manner.

(e) Spiritual gifts: the supremacy of love (12:1 − 14:40)

Another question which the Corinthians had raised in their letter to Paul was about spiritual gifts, with which they were abundantly endowed (1:7). How were these to be recognized, and how were they to be exercised? Evidently many members of the church attached most importance to the more ecstatic and spectacular manifestations of speaking with unknown tongues and prophesying—uttering unpremeditated words in which their hearers recognized the voice of the Spirit of God. But how could it be known that these utterances did come from the Spirit of God? By their content, says Paul, by the witness they bear to Christ. If they exalt him as Lord, then they are inspired by the Holy Spirit (12:1–3).

But there is a great variety of gifts in the church, some less spectacular than others, but all necessary for the proper functioning of the church as a living organism and all supplied by one and the same Spirit, by whom they have been made members of one body (12:4–13). (We should note the co-ordination of "the same Spirit...the same Lord...the same God" in 12:4–6, as a foreshadowing of later "trinitarian" statements of the doctrine of the Godhead.)

The test of the usefulness of the various gifts is the contribution which they make to the health of the body. A local church is the body of Christ; the individual Christians are parts of that body. If all the parts performed the same function, the result would be a monstrosity. But if each performs the function allotted to it by the Spirit, then the whole organism will be healthy and harmonious (12:14–31).

But one thing is necessary above all for this purpose, and that is the crowning gift of Christian charity, heavenly love. And so we come to chapter 13, the hymn of love. We may be talented, devoted, generous in our giving; we may be blessed with mountain-shifting faith; but all is in vain if love is absent. In his celebration of love Paul uses language which might well be used of Christ, if "Christ" were substituted for "love". Other spiritual gifts have their place for a time, but love endures for ever. Our present condition, in comparison with the perfection which we are to attain one day, is as childhood in comparison with the years of maturity. The things which belong to our present state of spiritual immaturity will be obsolete when we are glorified with Christ, but love will never grow obsolete. Faith, hope and love are graces which endure for ever; but love is the greatest of the three (13:1–13).

Love, then, should be pursued more than all the other spiritual qualities. But as regards the gifts that they were so interested in, prophecy—the declaration of the mind of God in the power of the Spirit—was one of prime importance. Speaking with unknown tongues, which the Corinthians appear to have valued most highly, was useful only when an interpreter was available. Paul himself has a larger endowment in this gift than all of them, but he would rather speak five intelligible words than ten thousand words in a language which his hearers did not understand (14:1–19).

What would a stranger think if he came into one of their meetings and heard them all speaking in strange languages? He would think they were all mad. But if he came in and heard them speaking by the power of the Spirit of God, he would be convicted by what he heard and acknowledge that God was in that place (14:20–25).

In short, the principle that they must follow in the exercise of varying gifts was mutual edification. If an utterance was not likely to be helpful to the members of the church, let it remain unuttered. And they should not all try to speak at once, or try to make room for as many utterances in "tongues" or acts of prophesying as possible. Let two or three speak at the most, one after another; the others should weigh what was being said. The proceedings must not be allowed to get out of rational control; the prophets should be equally able to speak and able to refrain from speaking. Anything in the nature of confusion does not come from God; he is a God of order and peace (14:26–33).

The injunction that women should keep quiet in church (14:34–36) is textually doubtful. In one group of early witnesses to the text it comes after verse 40. One explanation of this could be that it was a scribal note in the margin of a manuscript which later copyists incorporated in the text at different points. But other explanations are possible. If the injunction is genuine, the context implies that it was designed to discourage the interruption of prophetic utterances by the asking of untimely questions. It certainly does not limit women's authority to pray and prophesy, which has already been established in chapter 11.

Many of the details of this fourteenth chapter are inapplicable in most of our churches today, where prophesying and speaking with tongues are not everyday phenomena. But the "command of the Lord" through Paul to Corinth (14:37) is valid for churches of all ages, as it is summed up in the two injunctions: "Let all things be done for edification" (14:26) and "all things should be done decently and in order" (14:40).

(f) The resurrection faith (15:1–58)

The resurrection of the body was a Jewish doctrine which most of the Greeks found incredible and absurd. When Paul addressed the Athenian Areopagus, his audience listened to him patiently enough until he mentioned the resurrection of the dead, but at that point some of them began to scoff, while others put him off more politely (Acts 17:32). So at Corinth some of the better educated Christians looked on this element in the apostolic tradition as a rather crude accretion to the gospel which they would be better without. If, as they gathered from Paul, they had in one sense been raised from death with Christ in their baptism, they desired no other resurrection. The immortality of the soul was a perfectly respectable doctrine, and they could be quite content with that. Paul addresses himself to this situation in chapter 15, by pointing out that resurrection is basic to the gospel and to the salvation which those people owed to the gospel.

He reminds them first of all of the message which they had believed when first he came to Corinth: the message declared that the Christ who died and was buried rose again the third day and appeared to many witnesses, sometimes to a large number at a time (as to the 500 of verse 6, of whom the majority were alive to tell the tale when Paul was writing, twenty-five years later), at other times to individuals, like Peter, James and (last of all) Paul himself. It is noteworthy that Paul reckons the appearance of the risen Christ to himself on the Damascus road to be of the same order as his earlier appearances to his disciples during the forty days after his resurrection. Moreover, this basic message—Christ's death for his people's sins and his rising from the dead—was common to all the apostles; on these facts there was no divergence between Paul and the first followers of Jesus (15:11).

The doctrine of resurrection is thus essential to the

gospel. If there is no resurrection (as some Corinthian Christians were saying), then Christ could not have risen, and in that case the gospel was a hollow mockery and those who believed it were pitiable dupes (15:12–19). But the resurrection of Christ, in fact, was too well attested to be in doubt, and his resurrection guarantees the coming resurrection of his people, just as the first-fruits which were presented to God at Eastertide (Leviticus 23:9–11) guaranteed a plentiful harvest to follow. The resurrection-harvest will be followed by the eternal day of God, when all evil powers have been subdued by Christ and God is all in all (15:20–28).

It is the hope of resurrection-life, Paul goes on, that makes Christians take thought for their departed friends; it is the same hope that emboldens him and his fellow apostles to endure the dangers that they face in the service of Christ (15:29–34).

But if any, still incredulous, should ask how corpses can possibly rise again, Paul replies that, just as the present body is appropriate to its environment, so the resurrection body will be suited to a quite different environment. It will be a "spiritual body", whose wearers will participate in the glory of their risen Lord (15:35–50). The resurrection will take place when the last trumpet sounds (compare 1 Thessalonians 4:16), and in the same movement those who are still alive will be transformed from mortal beings into immortal ones. Death will then be finally abolished, through the single-handed victory of Christ. Here, surely, is ample encouragement for Christians to persevere in their service for Christ, knowing that it is not doomed to peter out in futility (15:51–58).

(g) The collection for Jerusalem (16:1–4)

The Corinthian Christians had heard that Paul was organizing a collection in his Gentile churches to be sent for the relief of the poverty-stricken church in Jerusalem, and in their letter they had asked what they should do about it. He tells them that week by week they should put some money aside for this purpose; then, when he came to Corinth, there would be no need for a hurried whip-round, for the money would be there, ready to be carried to Jerusalem by their own accredited envoys, probably accompanied by Paul himself.

5. Personal news (16:5–18)

Paul hopes to visit them next Pentecost (Whitsuntide); until then he will stay in Ephesus, where there are wonderful opportunities and encouragements for his apostolic ministry, in spite of the many opponents of the gospel (for one class of opponents see Acts 19:23 ff.). He urges them to make Timothy feel at home in their midst, so that he may come back to Paul with a good report. Paul had tried to persuade Apollos too to pay them a visit, but that would have to be deferred to a more convenient occasion. Quite clearly there was no personal animosity between Paul and Apollos.

The exhortation to be subject to the household of Stephanas, and to recognize along with him Fortunatus and Achaicus (16:15–18), suggests that even now, three years after Paul had left Corinth, the church there was without clearly-defined leaders. This was exceptional in a Pauline church and the reason must be a matter of speculation. Perhaps the qualities of leadership were slow in manifesting themselves in the Corinthian church; or the rank and file saw no reason for submitting to the guidance of others.

6. *Final greetings (16:19–24)*

Greetings are sent from the church in Ephesus and the other cities of the province of Asia; personal greetings are sent from Aquila and Prisca (Priscilla), who had been in Corinth during Paul's eighteen months there but were now with him in Ephesus. Paul adds his own greetings in his own hand. "Our Lord, come!" (verse 22) was a watchword in the early church, used especially at the end of the communion service, in its Aramaic form, *Marana-tha*.

5
The Ministry of Reconciliation: 2 Corinthians

THE PLAN OF 2 CORINTHIANS

A severe letter

WHEN THE letter which we know as 1 Corinthians was finished and taken to Corinth, it does not appear to have been as effective as might have been hoped with those elements in the church which were disaffected towards Paul, and Timothy would not be regarded as a strong enough representative to enforce the apostle's directions. The situation deteriorated, and a visit by Paul himself seemed necessary. But Paul's visit brought the opposition to a head. One party-leader in particular showed open hostility to him. Paul withdrew, and sent the church a letter, written with the full weight of his apostolic authority, in which he demanded that disciplinary action should be taken against those who refused his authority—or rather, the authority of the Lord whose ambassador he was. Titus, another of his colleagues, was the bearer of this letter, and after he set out upon his mission, Paul began to wonder whether possibly he had written too severely. He had left Ephesus by this time and attempted to carry on some missionary activity on the Asian shores of the Dardanelles, but he could not settle and set out for Macedonia. There Titus met him and reported that the letter had been a complete success. The church had been stung to such a degree of shame and indignation that, if anything, it was now in danger of going too far in its disciplinary action against the anti-Pauline faction.

The unbounded relief which this news brought to Paul is manifest throughout the earlier chapters of 2 Corinthians, which he wrote immediately on receiving the news. From these chapters, too, we can gather something of the character and the effect of the severe letter. Paul refers to it in 2 Corinthians 2:3–9 and again in 7:8–12.

A critical question

Has any part of this severe letter survived? Perhaps not. It cannot be identified with 1 Corinthians, and 2 Corinthians is the letter of relief and reconciliation which Paul wrote when Titus informed him how effective the severe letter had been. But it has been pointed out that there are some features in the last four chapters of 2 Corinthians which correspond remarkably to the description which Paul gives of the severe letter in the earlier chapters of the same epistle. There is, moreover, a very sharp and sudden change of tone as we pass from the ninth to the tenth chapter of 2 Corinthians. All this has led a number of scholars to the conclusion that what we call 2 Corinthians consists really of parts of two letters which Paul sent to the Corinthian church—chapters 10 to 13 representing the closing part of the severe letter and chapters 1 to 9 representing the opening part (probably everything except the final greetings) of the letter which he wrote after he received Titus's good news. This rearrangement would provide Paul's Corinthian correspondence (or at least all that survives of it in the New Testament) with a happy ending, but that is no argument in favour of the rearrangement: real life does not always work out that way.

If indeed parts of two separate letters of Paul to Corinth were put together by accident (and the burden of proof rests on those who maintain this view), they must have been put together about A.D. 100, when the collection of the scattered units of Paul's correspondence was being actively undertaken.

It is worth while comparing certain passages in chapters 10–13 with Paul's allusions to the severe letter in chapters 1–9. Compare, for example, 2 Corinthians 10:6 ("being ready to punish every disobedience, when your obedience is complete") with 2:9 ("this is why I wrote, that I might test you and know whether you are obedient in everything"); or 13:2 ("I warned those who sinned before and all the others, and I warn them now while absent... that if I come again I will not spare them") with 1:23 ("it was to spare you that I refrained from coming to Corinth"); or 13:10 ("I write this while I am away from you, in order that when I come I may not have to be severe") with 2:3 ("I wrote as I did, so that when I came I might not be pained by those who should have made me rejoice"); or 11:1 – 12:13 (where, speaking "as a fool", he boasts of his qualifications) with 3:1 ("Are we beginning to commend ourselves again?"). There are, to be sure, other allusions to the severe letter which have nothing corresponding to them in chapters 10–13, such as the case of the man who had led the opposition to Paul and whom Paul assures of his forgiveness in 2 Corinthians 2:5–11.

We should in any case have to suppose that a good part of the severe letter is lost, even if its closing section were preserved in 2 Corinthians 10–13. But there is one conclusive argument against identifying 2 Corinthians 10–13 with any part of the severe letter. That is the reference in 12:18 to a recent visit paid to Corinth by Titus, as Paul's messenger. The context of this reference shows that the visit by Titus must be that for which Paul prepares the church in 2 Corinthians 8:6, 16–24. Chapters 10–13 must therefore be later than chapters 1–9, the interval between chapters 9 and 10 being sufficient not only to allow Titus to reach Corinth and complete his business but also to allow time for a new situation to develop in the church there to account for the abrupt change of tone in 10:1. The mood of relief and reconciliation in chapters 1–9 gives way to vigorous remonstrance and irony in chapters 10–13.

Relief and reconciliation

In some ways, 2 Corinthians is the most revealing of all Paul's letters. When he wrote it, he had lately escaped from a great peril of which we should like to have more information than we have (1:8–11). Never in all his life had he been so near to death; in fact, he had given up all hope of life, and when in the event he was delivered from his dangerous plight he greeted his deliverance as a veritable resurrection, a miracle wrought by God. This experience evidently left a deep and permanent mark on him, so much so that some scholars have thought themselves able to decide from internal evidence on which side of this watershed in his life any one of his epistles should be placed. In this epistle we can probably trace the effect of his experience in his personal relations with his converts, in his reflection on the lot of an apostle, and in his references to the fuller life beyond the present one. He rejoices over his Corinthian friends, he assures them that he cherishes no personal resentment towards anyone for what has taken place, he promises to visit them again soon. The atmosphere of reconciliation which pervades the letter provides a congenial setting for a discussion of the ministry of reconciliation entrusted to preachers of the gospel. But Christian ideals must be realized in practice, and an opportunity for this presents itself in the collection which he is organizing to relieve the poverty of the Jerusalem church.

Outline of 2 Corinthians

A. Chapters 1–9

1. Salutation (1:1–2)
2. Thanksgiving for divine comfort (1:3–7)
3. His deliverance from deadly peril (1:8–11)
4. Explanation of his recent conduct towards them (1:12 – 2:17)
5. Old letter and new Spirit (3:1–18)
6. The glory and humiliation of apostleship (4:1–15)
7. The Christian hope (4:16 – 5:10)
8. The ministry of reconciliation (5:11 – 6:13)
9. Warning against pagan associations (6:14 – 7:1)
10. His confidence in the Corinthian Christians (7:2–16)
11. The collection for Jerusalem (8:1 – 9:15)

B. Chapters 10–13

1. Paul vindicates his apostolic authority (10:1–18)
2. He boasts "as a fool" (11:1–33)
3. A visionary experience and its lessons (12:1–10)
4. The signs of an apostle (12:11–13)
5. Reply to his critics and promise of a third visit (12:14 – 13:4)
6. Prayer for their improvement (13:5–10)
7. Final greetings and benediction (13:11–14)

EXPOSITION OF 2 CORINTHIANS

A. Chapters 1–9

1. *Salutation* (1:1–2)

As in the two Thessalonian letters (as well as Philippians, Colossians and Philemon), Timothy's name is conjoined with Paul's in the salutation. The other churches of Achaia are conjoined with the church of the chief city.

2. *Thanksgiving for divine comfort* (1:3–7)

Paul had passed through a very trying time, which was aggravated by his anxiety for the welfare and peace of the Corinthian church. The good news which he had just received from Titus was a very great comfort to him, and the theme of comfort introduced here pervades chapters 1–9 of this letter.

3. *His deliverance from deadly peril* (1:8–11)

The nature of the "affliction" which he had undergone in the province of Asia is not stated in so many words; his readers had probably heard something about it from Titus, and perhaps it was not politic to be too explicit about it in a letter which might fall into the wrong hands. It was probably more than a nearly fatal illness; it may well have involved prosecution on a serious charge in circumstances in which an appeal to

Caesar would have been worse than useless. Soon after Nero's accession to the imperial power in October, A.D. 54, the proconsul of Asia had been assassinated at the instance of Nero's mother. If Paul had earlier profited by the proconsul's protection during his ministry in Ephesus, this could now make him a marked man. At any rate, Paul found himself in a situation in which death seemed unavoidable, and when, contrary to all expectation, he escaped death, he greeted his deliverance from this deadly peril as nothing less than a resurrection, brought about by the power of God.

4. *Explanation of his recent conduct towards them* (1:12–2:17)

Relations had been strained between Paul and his Corinthian friends, but now that all was well between them once more he not only writes in a spirit of full reconciliation but wears his heart on his sleeve and tells them exactly why he has behaved as he has done recently. Some of them thought him vacillating and unable to make up his mind because he had altered his plans in some way in connection with a projected visit to Corinth. He assures them that his only reason for not coming, as he had arranged to do, was his desire to spare them pain. It was not that he was naturally fickle, saying "Yes" one day and "No" the next; that would be very unworthy behaviour on the part of a herald of the Christ who was himself the incarnate "Yes" to all the promises of God. Instead of paying them a visit which, in the circumstances, was bound to be painful, he wrote them a letter. It caused him pain to write it, and he knew it would cause them pain to read it; but his purpose in writing it was that they might know how greatly he loved and cared for them.

There was one man at Corinth in particular who had caused Paul sorrow (2:5); perhaps he had opposed him to the point of publicly insulting him. When Paul wrote, he demanded that the church should show whether it approved of this man's conduct or not; and his letter filled them with such shame and remorse that they were now in danger of going too far in the discipline which they imposed on this erring brother. Paul now cries "Enough!" and tells them that it is time to restore the offender to full fellowship and assure him of their love. The personal terms of forgiveness which Paul uses (2:10) suggest that the man was guilty of a personal injury against Paul; this rules out the view that he was the excommunicated man of 1 Corinthians 5.

Paul goes on to tell them that, after he sent them his painful letter, he could not rest in his mind or settle to any course of action until he knew what its effect was, in spite of the opportunity for gospel witness which presented itself in Troas (Asia Minor). He crossed into Macedonia, in order the sooner to meet Titus who was on his way back from Corinth after delivering the letter there (2:12, 13). But when he met Titus in Macedonia, what joy, what relief, what exultation in Christ! Christ had triumphed in his people, and a situation which could only have brought discredit to his name was overcome. Paul, the servant of Christ, was wholeheartedly recognized by the whole Corinthian church as a true apostle, and not as someone who made merchandise of the gospel for his own profit (2:14–17).

5. *Old letter and new Spirit* (3:1–18).

The vindication of Paul's apostleship leads him to enlarge on the dignity of this ministry to which Christ has called him. Not that he has any thought of asserting his apostolic claims all over again. Emissaries from the Jerusalem church to the Gentile churches brought "letters of commendation" with them, signed by Jerusalem leaders; but Paul was not reduced to the necessity of being commended by others to his own converts, who in fact were his own living "letter of commendation"—a "letter from Christ" attesting his apostleship, not engraved on stone tablets like the Ten Commandments but in the hearts of men and women (3:1–3).

The Ten Commandments formed the basis of the old covenant of Moses' day (compare Exodus 24:7), but Christ's new covenant, which Paul and his fellow apostles had the privilege of administering, was made effective by the Holy Spirit. The old law on the tablets of stone proclaimed death to those who infringed it, but the Spirit is the giver of life. And yet the inauguration of the old covenant was attended by manifestations of divine glory; how much more glorious, then, was the new covenant which came to supersede it!

The apostles were thus invested with greater honour

than Moses, the mediator of the old covenant; for theirs was the task of announcing the new and eternal covenant. Moses' face shone when he came down from his interview with God on Mount Sinai, so much so that he was compelled to veil his face (Exodus 34:29–35). That veil, by a transference of thought, is viewed by Paul as still obscuring the vision of those Jews who had not recognized Christ for what he was; but it is removed when a man turns to the Lord—that is the Spirit, says Paul—and he not only sees clearly but enjoys a freedom which the old law could never permit. In the old age one man spoke with God face to face (Exodus 33:11); but under the new covenant all believers have free access to God and are able to see his glory revealed in Christ. Not only so, but thanks to the activity of the Spirit of God they reflect the divine glory which they see—not temporarily, like Moses, but in an ever increasing degree, becoming more and more like their Lord (3:4–18).

6. *The glory and humiliation of apostleship* (4:1–15)

Was it not a high honour to be entrusted with so glorious a gospel as this? Who could lose heart when assured of the enabling grace of the almighty Spirit? And who could stoop to use unworthy means to further the cause of so pure and holy a Lord? Underhand methods in any case could never accomplish the work of God. There was nothing obscure about the gospel; if any obscurity accompanied its preaching, that was the work of "the god of this world" (that is the devil, the chief adversary of God and man), keeping a veil on the eyes of unbelieving hearers, blinding their minds against the divine light. But where the divine light was accepted, a new creation sprang into being. In the Genesis narrative, creation began when God said "Let there be light"—and there was light. So when the gospel is believed, the light of God shining in the face of Christ illuminates the human heart, and a new creation begins. The message which brings this to pass is rightly called "the gospel of the glory of Christ"; for it is Christ, the "likeness of God", who manifests the glory of God to all who enter the new covenant (4:1–6).

Yet who, to look at the apostles, would suppose that they were entrusted with so glorious a ministry? They were frail, weak men, exposed to mortal danger day by day. In them, as in receptacles of common earthenware, the heavenly treasure was deposited, so that no one would make the mistake of confounding the treasure with the plain container. They themselves were nothing; the gospel committed to their charge was everything. Paul's recent experiences at Ephesus have left their mark on him; he speaks as one for whom death is a familiar companion—but it is death for Jesus' sake, or rather it is a sharing in the very death of Jesus, which brings with it the sharing of his resurrection life as well. And he endures all this for his converts' sake, assured that on the day of resurrection he and they together will appear in the presence of their risen Lord, so that God will be glorified (4:7–15).

7. *The Christian hope* (4:16 – 5:10)

This expectation fills Paul and his fellow apostles with good courage. The trouble and distress attendant upon their gospel ministry, severe as it might be, was but a light burden to bear compared with the incomparable "weight of glory" to which they could look forward. (The expression "weight of glory" may have come naturally to one brought up on the Hebrew Bible, where one word does duty for both "weight" and "glory".) The affliction, lifelong though it might be, was a momentary experience compared with the eternity of the coming glory; indeed, in some sense the affliction was actually producing the coming glory. So Paul kept his eyes on what was eternal rather than on what was momentary. The outward shell might waste away, but a new nature was coming to maturity within (2 Corinthians 4:16 was a message which Dr. Martin Niemöller sent to his wife from the concentration camp where he was held as Hitler's personal prisoner). And one day soon the outward shell would be discarded; the tent would be taken down and folded up. But a new dwelling, an immortal body, was even now being prepared by God, ready to replace the old one (4:16 – 5:1).

It is no disembodied existence that Paul longs for, but one in which he will wear his heavenly body and enjoy the believer's heritage of glory in the presence of the Lord. He regards the indwelling Spirit as providing here and now the guarantee of what awaits him in the life to come. A disembodied state, bereft of all means of communication with one's environment, was something from which his imagination shrank. Such a state might be an unwelcome necessity, between death and resurrection; although here one could well believe that Paul expects the new body to be ready for his wearing as soon as he puts off the old one. Best of all would it be if the mortal body were even now transformed and "swallowed up by life", without passing through death. But if, as seemed likely, he must pass through death, that would simply mean being "away from the body and at home with the Lord". One way or the other, the judgment seat of Christ must be faced, and therefore Paul's present concern was to please Christ (5:2–10).

8. *The ministry of reconciliation* (5:11 – 6:13)

Accordingly his apostolic service was discharged from no motives of self-advertisement or desire for men's approval; it was by the joint constraint of "the fear of the Lord" and "the love of Christ" (two things which go naturally together) that he preached the gospel and proclaimed God's message of reconciliation in Christ. The Christ whom he preached was no longer assessed by Paul according to his former standards of human wisdom; he had come to know him as the risen and exalted Lord, who created anew all those who were "in him"—those who by faith-union with him shared his resurrection life. It was in this Christ that God undertook to reconcile the world to himself, and the apostles were his ambassadors, announcing his amnesty for Christ's sake (5:11–21).

The Corinthian Christians have listened to these ambassadors, and have accepted God's gracious amnesty proclaimed by them; let them see to it that they have not accepted it in vain. Paul and his fellow ambassadors had behaved towards them with the utmost sincerity, enduring no end of discomfort and danger in order to bring God's blessing to others; it was only reasonable that they should expect to be requited with sincerity and grateful affection on the part of their converts. Paul therefore asks them to make room for him in their hearts, as they have a warm place in his (6:1–13).

9. *Warning against pagan associations* (6:14–7:1)

Some commentators feel that this short section breaks the continuity of Paul's argument, and that what we have here is a fragment of the letter to which he refers in 1 Corinthians 5:9–11, in which he warned them not to keep company with immoral people. Others have pointed to affinities between these verses and strongly separatist passages in Qumran literature. But Paul is quite capable of digressing in his argument, and it could be that the earnestness of his plea for open-heartedness immediately before and after this section arises from his converts' proneness to compromise with idolatry, thus ignoring his instructions and behaving as though they had accepted the divine amnesty "in vain". "Belial" (6:15) is the personal embodiment of wickedness, here practically the same as "Antichrist". The general tone of the indignant questions in 6:14–16 suggests that some of his readers had not laid to heart the warning of 1 Corinthians 10:14 ff. against becoming "partners with demons" by attending idolatrous banquets in pagan temples. He begs them anew to have done with all such defiling associations and go on to perfect holiness.

10. *His confidence in the Corinthian Christians* (7:2–16)

He does not go on in this admonitory vein, however, because he is so full of gratitude and relief at his recent complete reconciliation with his Corinthian friends. They have affirmed their loyalty to him; he now affirms his confidence in them. His joy and comfort know no bounds, and again he tells them of the thankfulness with which he received Titus's news in Macedonia (compare 2:13). After he had sent Titus to them with his severe letter, he was sorry he had done so; but when Titus came back and told him of the effect of the letter, he could no longer regret having written it. They had not really meant to hurt Paul, and when his letter showed them how deeply they had in fact hurt him, they were only too anxious to prove to him how sorry they were for this and how angry they were with the individual who had taken the lead in opposing him. Paul, moreover, had told Titus (hoping against hope, perhaps) when he sent him to Corinth that the Corinthian Christians were loyal and loving at heart, and their reaction to the severe letter showed Titus how true was Paul's assessment of them. Here too Paul had cause for renewed gladness and confidence in them.

11. *The collection for Jerusalem* (8:1–9:15)

In 1 Corinthians 16:1–4 Paul had already told them how he wished them to proceed with the collection which he was organizing in his churches for their fellow Christians in Jerusalem. A year had gone by since then, and it was necessary to say something more about it, partly because some of his detractors were misrepresenting his motives in this connection. He tells them first how generous and spontaneous has been the response by the Macedonian churches (in particular, no doubt, those in Philippi and Thessalonica). Poor as they were, they had given not merely according to what they had but beyond it; their devotion in this was but a token of the devotion with which they had given themselves to Christ. Paul uses their example to encourage the Corinthian Christians to persevere in laying money aside for this purpose. But theirs is not the only example he adduces: Christians should find their supreme incentive to generosity and self-sacrifice in the example of Christ, who impoverished himself for his people's infinite enrichment. Let the Corinthians, then, who are rich as compared with their Macedonian brethren, give from their abundance as the Macedonians had given from their poverty (8:1–15).

Paul is about to send Titus back to them to complete the arrangements for the Corinthian contribution, and with him he is sending two other Christian men who had already discharged delicate responsibilities of this kind to the satisfaction of other churches. One of these, "the brother whose praise is in the gospel throughout all the churches" (8:18, Authorized Version), has been traditionally identified with Luke the physician, but his identity is quite uncertain. It is clear that Paul took every care that financial negotiations in which he was involved should be carried out in a way that would stand up to the keenest scrutiny; none of his detractors should be able to find any fault with him on this score (8:16–24).

He tells the Corinthians that he has been encouraging other churches to contribute generously and promptly by citing the example of Achaia, the province of which Corinth was the chief city; I know, he says, that you won't let me down. But the contribution should be made willingly and cheerfully, not grudgingly. It is a gift to God, and God will be no one's debtor. Moreover, as an act of Christian fellowship it will lead to the forging of firmer bonds between the Jerusalem Christians and the Gentile churches; they will all pray for one another more earnestly and effectively in consequence. All Christian giving is a reflection of the grace of God, in giving the greatest gift of all (9:1–15).

B. Chapters 10–13

1. *Paul vindicates his apostolic authority* (10:1–18)

The sharp change of tone at the beginning of chapter 10 calls for some explanation. Paul has just received further news from Corinth which indicates that the reconciliation is not so complete as he has been led to believe. It can be inferred that visitors, probably from Judaea, had intruded into Paul's mission field and had won some success in prejudicing the minds of his Corinthian converts against him. They called his apostolic authority in question and appealed to the superior authority of men whom they called "superlative apostles" or "top apostles"—Peter, possibly, with some others of the twelve apostles, and James the brother of Jesus. We need not suppose that they had the authority of Peter and James for invoking them in this way, but they seem, possibly on their own initiative, to have embarked on a campaign to bring Paul's churches under the control of the Jerusalem church and its leaders.

In belittling Paul's apostolic status they pointed to his lack of self-assertiveness and criticized him freely: "He won't say 'Boo' to a goose when he is here himself", they said; "but when he is away he pretends to be bold and fearless and writes strong letters; if he were sure of his authority, he would show some of his letter-writing severity when he is dealing with us face to face." He replies that if his writing does not bring them to their senses, they will see just how severe he can be in their presence. Unlike certain other people he does not assert his authority in churches which he has not planted himself, but the Corinthian Christians are his converts and ought to recognize his authority. Yet self-praise is no honour, and he is much more anxious to have the Lord's approval than to assert his own authority.

2. He boasts "as a fool" (11:1–33)

For Paul in fact found it extremely distasteful to have to defend his claims to be recognized as an apostle, especially to people who themselves provided the clearest evidence of his apostleship. Yet something had to be said; they were so ready to pay heed to others who came in their own name and tried to seduce them from their true allegiance, "false apostles" whose claims upon their attention could not be compared with Paul's. Even Paul's practice of earning his own living to avoid becoming a financial burden to his converts was counted against him: he would certainly require them to support him, it was said, if he were confident of his right to do so. These interlopers evidently had no qualms about living at the Corinthian Christians' expense, and they in turn were evidently quite willing to put up with this imposition. And yet these people could boast of no qualifications to compare with Paul's.

Boasting was a foolish game, he felt, but if he was compelled to join in it he had something to boast about. The catalogue of his afflictions in verses 23–27 shows that *The Acts of the Apostles* provides only a selection from the record of his adventures. Of his frequent imprisonments (11:23) we know of only one up to the time when he was writing to the Corinthians: that was at Philippi (Acts 16:23). Where else was he imprisoned? Very probably in Ephesus, where he had just spent the best part of three years, and it was very probably at Ephesus, too, that he had been "often near death" (compare 1 Corinthians 15:32, 2 Corinthians 1:8–10). We should like to know the circumstances of his five floggings at the hands of Jewish authorities, but no further details have been preserved to us. We have details of only one of the three beatings with rods which he mentions in verse 25; that, like the imprisonment already referred to, was at Philippi (Acts 16:22 f.). The stoning mentioned in the same verse took place at Lystra (Acts 14:19). We know nothing further about the shipwrecks which he mentions in the second part of the verse; the shipwreck off Malta (Acts 27:39 – 28:1) took place some four years after this. Yet the care of his converts gave him more anxiety than anything else.

An impressive list indeed! Who could read it and question Paul's apostolic claims? Yet he soon grows tired of such boasting and says he prefers to boast of things which one might well wish to cover up—as when he had to be let down in a basket through a window in the city wall of Damascus to escape his enemies' attention (compare Acts 9:23–25). A memory like that would save him from becoming too boastful!

3. *A visionary experience and its lessons* (12:1–10)

Some people boasted about visions and revelations that had been granted to them; why should not Paul do likewise? So he recounts a strange experience which must have come to him at Tarsus, before he joined Barnabas at Syrian Antioch (Acts 11:25 f.). He had an ecstatic vision of the paradise above, the third heaven, during which he heard things which must not be spoken. Such experiences are by no means unparalleled, however abnormal they may seem to be to western Protestants to-day. Was not that something to boast about, even if it was frustrating not to be able to put the details of the vision into words? But the experience was followed by a recurring physical affliction so disagreeable, so humiliating, that Paul earnestly prayed for its removal. It was not removed, but he was given added strength to endure it. We cannot be sure what this "thorn in the flesh" really was—epilepsy, malaria, ophthalmia or a speech impediment have been among the suggested diagnoses—but it was evidently something that made Paul fear that his usefulness as a servant of Christ was at an end. He learned, however, to rejoice in it, even to boast of it, because it had taught him so much more of the power of God's grace in his life: "when I am weak, then I am strong."

4. *The signs of an apostle* (12:11–13)

A truce to boasting! Why should Paul have to defend his apostleship among his own converts? The "superlative apostles" had to exaggerate their credentials; Paul required only to remind his readers of what they themselves had seen and heard when he was with them—the unmistakable marks of a true messenger of Christ. Had he treated the Corinthian church differently from any of his other churches—or had he perhaps wronged them by refusing to live at their expense? (Perhaps they felt, indeed, that they had been wronged in this, because it might have looked as if he had not as much confidence in them as in some of his other churches.)

5. *Reply to his critics and promise of a third visit* (12:14 – 13:4)

Paul's second visit to Corinth, of which we have no detailed record, must be reconstructed by inferences from remarks in his correspondence with Corinth; but it had not been a happy one. He proposed to pay them a third visit; it was for them to decide whether this would be a happier occasion than the last visit.

Were they still complaining that he refused to live at their expense? No matter; he would not change this policy. After all, he was their spiritual father, and parents ought to provide for their children, not children for their parents. But what of those who said that his refusal to live at their expense was just a façade—that he was exploiting them in other and more subtle ways, through Titus or those other messengers, for example, whom he sent to collect money for his Jerusalem scheme? That some of his detractors were saying this about him seems plain. His answer is simply to invite the Corinthian Christians to speak from their own experience; they knew very well that neither Titus nor any other messenger of Paul's behaved towards them any differently from Paul himself.

They must not think that in all this Paul's own vindication has been his primary concern. Far from it; although he may have appeared to be defending himself, he has really been writing with the view of helping them to see the situation in its proper perspective, to repent of their perverse behaviour, so that when he pays them his third visit there will be no repetition of the disgraceful and humiliating attack on him that had marred his former visit. But if in fact there is no repentance, then they may be sure that he will assert his apostolic authority unsparingly when he comes.

6. *Prayer for their improvement* (13:5–10)

He urges them to consider whether in fact they are still maintaining the original purity and sincerity of their faith. Or can it be that, having begun to run the Christian race, they must be disqualified? (That is the sense of "fail to meet the test"—"be reprobates", says the Authorized Version—in verse 5.) No; he has better hopes of them than that, so he prays for their improvement. Anyone who believes that "we cannot do anything against the truth, but only for the truth" (verse 8) will be saved from anxiety and panic in his endeavour to defend the truth.

7. *Final greetings and benediction* (13:11–14)

So he bids them farewell, with a final admonition. The apostolic benediction with which the letter ends shows how early the trinitarian faith entered the thinking of early Christians. Its spontaneity of expression is more impressive than a deliberate formula would be.

* * * * * *

We do not know what immediate effect this sharp remonstrance had. Some of Paul's friends in Corinth certainly remained faithful to him; for example, he spent three winter months in A.D. 56–57 as the guest of Gaius, who at an early date in Paul's evangelization of Corinth had put his home at the disposal of the infant church there (Romans 16:23).

But forty years after 2 Corinthians was written there was still a spirit of unruliness among the Christians of Corinth, and a further remonstrance had to be sent to them—this time from the sister-church of Rome (through its foreign secretary Clement), which appears to have taken over something of Paul's responsibility in the churches of his former mission field.

6
A Call for Unity: Philippians

THE PLAN OF PHILIPPIANS

The gospel comes to Philippi

In A.D. 50 Paul and three companions—Silvanus (Silas), Timothy and Luke—set sail from the port of Alexandria Troas, in north-west Asia Minor, and crossed the North Aegean in response to the call which Paul had heard in a night-vision: "Come over to Macedonia and help us" (Acts 16:9). They landed at Neapolis (modern Kavalla) and travelled inland for about ten miles until they came to Philippi.

Philippi bore the name of Philip II, king of Macedonia (father of Alexander the Great), who founded it in 356 B.C. on a site earlier called Krenides ("fountains"). With the rest of Macedonia, it was incorporated into the Roman Empire in 146 B.C. The Romans built a great highway across Macedonia from east to west, linking the Adriatic Sea with the North Aegean. It was called the Egnatian Road; Philippi lay on it, near its eastern terminus. At Philippi in 42 B.C. a decisive battle was fought in which the army led by the assassins of Julius Caesar (Brutus and Cassius) was defeated by the followers of his heir Octavian (later the Emperor Augustus) and of his chief lieutenant Mark Antony. The victors settled many of their veteran soldiers there and gave the city a new constitution as a Roman colony (Luke draws attention to its status when he introduces Philippi in Acts 16:12). A Roman colony had the same kind of municipal administration as the city of Rome: Philippi was governed by two collegiate magistrates called praetors, and they were attended by police officials called lictors.

On their arrival in Philippi Paul and his companions preached the gospel and made a number of converts, although Paul and Silvanus incurred the ill-will of some Philippian citizens, who laid a charge against them before the praetors; in consequence, they suffered the indignity of being beaten with the lictors' rods and locked up for a night in the town jail. But the upshot of this was that the jailer was converted to Christianity. Another of their converts in Philippi—their first, indeed—was Lydia, from Thyatira in Asia Minor, who traded in the purple dye (manufactured from the juice of the madder root) for which her native place was famous. She extended the hospitality of her home to the missionaries during their stay in the city. Luke's account of the evangelization of Philippi might almost have been designed to illustrate the wide variety of types who found their need met by the gospel.

A bond of warm affection was forged between Paul

and the Christians of Philippi. They kept in touch with him, and played a full part in contributing to the relief fund which he organized for the church of Jerusalem. He appears to have visited them more than once in the course of his later movements.

The occasion of the letter

After the winter of A.D. 56–57, which Paul spent at Corinth as the guest of his friend and convert Gaius, he made plans to travel to Jerusalem to supervise the delivery of the relief fund to the leaders of the mother church. It was his wish that delegates of the contributing churches should go with him to hand over their own churches' contributions, and a number of them joined him in Corinth on the eve of embarkation: their names are listed in Acts 20:4. The majority of them set sail from Corinth. Paul went north to Philippi, however, and embarked on another ship there, in the company of Luke; they met up with the rest of the party at Troas and continued their voyage to Judaea.

Not many days after they arrived in Jerusalem, Paul was attacked by a hostile crowd in the temple precincts and was snatched from his assailants by members of the Roman garrison, from its adjacent headquarters. The commander of the garrison took him into custody and sent him to Caesarea for greater security. The Jewish hierarchy lodged an accusation against him before the Roman governor of Judaea for violation of the sanctity of the temple and other alleged offences. After two years of dilatoriness on the part of the Roman authorities, Paul exercised his right as a Roman citizen and appealed to have his case heard at Rome by the emperor. To Rome, then, he was sent and, having arrived there early in A.D. 60, he spent two years under house arrest, waiting for his appeal to come before the imperial tribunal.

While he was in Rome, his friends in Philippi sent him a gift of money by the hand of Epaphroditus, one of their number. Paul sent a letter to thank them for the gift, to let them know his present situation and his immediate prospects, and to give them the kind of encouragement he knew they would find helpful.

Outline of Philippians

1. Salutation, thanksgiving and intercessory prayer (1:1–11)
2. Paul's present situation (1:12–26)
3. Encouragement to endurance, unity and witness:
   (a) Endurance in face of opposition (1:27–30)
   (b) Appeal for unity (2:1–5)
   (c) The song of Christ's glory (2:6–11)
   (d) Call to Christian witness (2:12–18)
4. Timothy and Epaphroditus:
   (a) Timothy and his devoted service (2:19–24)
   (b) Epaphroditus and his serious illness (2:25–30)
   (c) First conclusion: call to rejoice (3:1)
5. Warning and encouragement:
   (a) Warning against legalists (3:2, 3)
   (b) Paul's aim in life (3:4–16)
   (c) Warning against libertines (3:17–19)

(d) Citizens of heaven (3:20, 21)
(e) Plea for faithfulness, harmony, joy and peace (4:1–7)
(f) Food for thought; second conclusion (4:8, 9)
6. Thanks for a gift (4:10–20)
7. Final greetings and benediction (4:21–23)

EXPOSITION OF PHILIPPIANS

1. *Salutation, thanksgiving and intercessory prayer* (1:1–11)

Paul regularly adds Timothy's name to his own in the opening salutation when Timothy is with him at the time of writing. The church of Philippi, which is saluted along with its "bishops and deacons", was clearly better administered and therefore, no doubt, more orderly than the church of Corinth.

Paul assures the Philippian Christians of his unfeigned gratitude and affection for them, because the remembrance of them brought him so much joy. While he is under guard, awaiting trial, he knows that they are with him in spirit. He prays that the Christian graces which are already so manifest in them will go on increasing until they reach full fruition on the day when Christ is revealed.

2. *Paul's present situation* (1:12–26)

Paul's present situation, he tells his readers, has

been working out for the advance of the gospel; it has made the cause of Christ a public talking-point. The soldiers of the praetorian guard, the emperor's personal bodyguard, who have been put in charge of Paul, know that it is for the sake of the gospel that he is in their custody, and Paul sees to it that they know what the gospel is. The Roman Christians have seized the opportunity to spread the gospel with redoubled vigour. Some of them do so in a spirit of unity with Paul. But there are others who disapprove of him and his mission and hope that he will feel frustrated and resentful at the thought of their activity while he has to remain inactive. But not he! So long as the gospel is preached, the preachers' motives are of minor importance: "Christ is proclaimed, and in that I rejoice" (verse 18).

In law Paul is Caesar's prisoner; from his own point of view he is Christ's soldier, currently posted in Rome "for the defence of the gospel" (verse 16). He has reason to believe that his case will soon come up for hearing in the imperial court, and his main concern is that, when the time comes for him to make his defence, he will speak in such a way as to magnify Christ. His court appearance will give him an unparalleled opportunity of declaring the gospel at the heart of the empire. He cannot foresee whether the outcome of the hearing will be acquittal or conviction (which would probably involve the death sentence). If it were the latter, it would be greatly to his advantage to be released from mortal life and be with Christ. But his friends are praying hard for his acquittal, and he knows that it will be better for them if he is spared to them for a little longer, so he thinks it more probable that their prayers will be answered and he will be released.

3. *Encouragement to endurance, unity and witness*

(a) *Endurance in face of opposition* (1:27–30)

Meanwhile, he urges them to maintain their Christian loyalty and preserve unbroken unity in their witness. They have their opponents, and so has Paul. This is inevitable when people are engaged in a contest: let the opposition remind them that he and they are engaged in the same contest for the cause of Christ.

(b) *Appeal for unity* (2:1–5)

He has urged them to preserve unbroken unity in their Christian witness, but from news that he has received about them he gathers that their unity is not so deep-rooted and complete as he should wish to see. He begs them to think and feel alike, and so fill his cup of joy to the full. Humility, not pride or self-esteem, should characterize them; let them honour others rather than seek honour themselves, and promote others' interests in preference to their own. They could all share a common mind if they all shared the mind of Christ.

(c) *The song of Christ's glory* (2:6–11)

The mind of Christ was celebrated in the words of a primitive hymn or confession with which they were probably familiar. How was his mind revealed? Not by getting but by giving; not by self-aggrandizement but by self-emptying. He did not exploit for his own advantage the divine nature which was his from the beginning; he humbled himself by becoming man and living on earth in the service of others. In him the form of God was perfectly displayed, and it was displayed in the form of a servant. More than that: in obedience to God he followed the path that led to the vilest of deaths—death by crucifixion. Humiliation could go no lower. But because he humbled himself God exalted him: the name high over all is his. It is God's good pleasure that all, in hell or earth or sky, should bend the knee at Jesus' name and confess that he is Lord.

(d) Call to Christian witness (2:12–18)

Again Paul urges his Philippian friends to cultivate a spirit of unity and lead blameless lives. They are God's children; let them conduct themselves accordingly, so that others may see their heavenly Father's grace in them. Then they will shine like lamps in the darkness of the surrounding world: the light they display will be the message of life—the gospel. Their faithfulness will be an acceptable sacrifice to God, and if something further is required to make their sacrifice complete, Paul is willing that his life should be poured out as a libation on top of their sacrifice. If, after all, he is called upon to undergo martyrdom, let it be reckoned to their credit, not to his own.

4. *Timothy and Epaphroditus*

(a) *Timothy and his devoted service* (2:19–24)

As soon as he knows how things are turning out for him he will send Timothy to Philippi with the news. Later he hopes to pay them a visit in person. They will be glad to see Timothy, who has served him with unequalled devotion. They had seen Timothy over ten years before, when he had only recently joined Paul. During the intervening years he had helped Paul selflessly, caring for him as a son might care for a father. The Philippian Christians will find Timothy a completely congenial visitor, likeminded with Paul himself; they will find that he shares Paul's own affectionate concern for their well-being.

(b) *Epaphroditus and his illness* (2:25–30)

Meanwhile Paul is sending Epaphroditus back to them. Epaphroditus was one of their own number, whom they had recently sent to Paul with a gift. But the journey (which would have lasted about forty days) took its toll of Epaphroditus; he fell ill and was at death's door for a time. The Philippians wanted him to stay on with Paul and give him the kind of personal service that they would all have been glad to render had it been possible; and Epaphroditus himself was anxious to do so. But Paul knew that the sooner Epaphroditus was back home in Philippi the better it would be for him, so he insisted that he should return, probably taking this letter with him. In the letter Paul makes it plain to the Philippians that he takes full responsibility for sending Epaphroditus back. He commends Epaphroditus to them as the kind of person who is worthy of special honour in the church. Timothy and Epaphroditus, in fact, showed themselves to have no small measure of the mind of Christ—and the same might be said of Paul himself.

(c) First conclusion: call to rejoice (3:1)

"Finally, my brethren," says Paul, and we may think the letter is coming to an end. It may be, indeed, that in Philippians 3:2 – 4:9 we have a series of warnings and encouragements from an earlier letter of Paul to the Philippians, inserted into the larger letter when Paul's literary remains were being collected and prepared for publication. But there can be no certainty about this.

"Rejoice in the Lord" is a recurring keynote of the letter to the Philippians.

5. Warning and encouragement

(a) Warning against legalists (3:2, 3)

Quite suddenly (it appears) Paul launches into a stern warning against some people whom he regards as workers of iniquity. His fierce language about them is as seething as his denunciation of the "false apostles" of 2 Corinthians 11:13, and it is probably men of the same type who are in view here. Because they stress the importance of circumcision, he calls them the mutilation party; for him the true circumcision is the inward cleansing effected in the people of God by his Spirit.

Those trouble-makers have not come to Philippi yet, so far as Paul knows; but they may do so, and he puts the church on its guard against them.

(b) Paul's aim in life (3:4–16)

As in 2 Corinthians 11:21, 22, Paul remarks that, if he were disposed to boast about his heritage and achievements, as those trouble-makers do, he could produce much more impressive credentials than theirs; but he mentions a few of them only to dismiss them as being now no better than street-sweepings by comparison with what he has found in Christ.

Once Paul's ambition had been to win God's acceptance by achieving perfection in the righteousness prescribed by the Jewish law. But since then he had learned to appreciate the new way of righteousness provided by God in the gospel and now he knows himself justified by faith in Christ. God's acceptance of him is no longer something to be earned by personal effort or merit. It has been bestowed on him by heavenly grace; he is accepted in Christ. His ambition is now to increase in the personal knowledge of Christ, sharing the sufferings of Christ in his own body, experiencing his risen power, ultimately accepting death as he did and attaining resurrection with him. Total likeness to Christ, the climax of perfection, he has not yet achieved, nor will he, so long as he remains in mortal body. But this is what he aims at, straining every effort to reach it, running straight towards it like an athlete striving to win a race, so that one day he may be called up by God to receive the prize. And what could the prize be but that total likeness to Christ at which he aims, knowing him as he himself is known?

Let those who are spiritually mature share the same aim. If there are some who cannot yet make this their single aim, or appreciate what this aim involves, God will reveal it to them. He is gracious and patient with those who wish to do his will. More guidance will be given them as they live according to the light they have already received, following the example of Paul and his associates.

(c) Warning against libertines (3:17–19)

There are many itinerant teachers who provide no safe example to follow. Paul, with a conscience that is clear in the presence of God, can recommend his own example, but he thinks of some (not necessarily in Philippi) who live as though the gospel gave them licence to indulge in sin and who encourage others to do the same. The readers are warned against those libertines—"enemies of the cross of Christ", as Paul calls them—just as, at the opposite extreme, they have been warned against the legalists. It was not only at Corinth that Paul had to wage war on two fronts.

(d) Citizens of heaven (3:20, 21)

But believers in Christ should live as befits citizens of heaven: their true home is where their Saviour is. (The implication may be that, as Philippi was a colony of Rome, so each Christian community is a colony of heaven.) It is from their true home that they expect their Saviour to appear, to transform their present bodies of mortal clay until they share the glory of his resurrection body. With this prospect in view, Paul encourages his readers to stand firm in the Lord.

(e) Plea for faithfulness, harmony, joy and peace (4:1–7)

Into this renewed plea Paul introduces a personal note: he appeals by name to two women, Euodia and Syntyche, to agree as Christians should. He evidently knows them well enough to be confident that they will not resent being singled out thus. He adds words of warm appreciation of their strenuous co-operation with him in his gospel ministry: "they contended side by side with me", he says (verse 3), using the same form of words as he has done with reference to their church as a whole in 1:27. It would be interesting to know the identity of the "true yokefellow" whom he asks to help these two women: perhaps it was Luke.

Because the Lord is always at hand, they need have no anxiety: God's peace will stand garrison over their hearts.

(f) Food for thought: second conclusion (4:8, 9)

Let them feed their minds with all that is pure, noble and lovely. The subject-matter of one's thoughts gives character to life. Let them follow Paul's teaching and example: how careful he must have been to avoid leading any of his converts astray by any word or action of his! By aiming at the highest in thought and life, they will have not only the peace of God but the God of peace himself.

6. *Thanks for a gift* (4:10–20)

Now he thanks the Philippians for the gift they have sent him with Epaphroditus. He recalls their generosity in earlier days, immediately after he first preached the gospel to them: they sent him gifts both when he left Philippi for Thessalonica, and also after that, when he left Macedonia and settled in Corinth. But for some years now they have "lacked opportunity" to do so. How? Because he himself had deprived them of any such opportunity by asking that all their giving should be channelled into the Jerusalem relief fund. But now that relief fund was closed; the money raised had been taken to Jerusalem. Paul was now in circumstances where he was unable to earn his own livelihood (it would have been difficult to carry on the work of tentmaking while he was handcuffed to a Roman soldier). The Philippians' care for him, which was never absent, has flourished anew now that the opportunity of making a personal gift to him has returned. Paul expresses appreciation of their gift, and even more of the spirit in which it has been made; he assures them that, as they have looked after his needs, God will look after theirs.

7. *Final greetings and benediction* (4:21–23)

He sends them all his greetings, with greetings also from his companions and from the Christians of Rome, especially from Christian members of the imperial household—slaves, freedmen and other retainers, from some of whom the emperor's civil service was staffed. Then he ends his letter with the grace.

* * *

Despite his concern for their unity of spirit, the church of Philippi caused Paul less anxiety than most of his churches did. Fifty years later it shows the same character as is reflected in Paul's letter. About A.D. 110 Ignatius, bishop of Antioch in Syria, passed through Philippi as he was being taken to Rome under armed guard to suffer a martyr's death in the arena. The Christians of Philippi evidently did what they could to ease his hardships during his brief stopover in their city, and became so interested in him that they wrote to Polycarp, bishop of Smyrna, to ask for copies of letters which they knew Ignatius had sent to him and to other Christians in the province of Asia. Polycarp did what they asked, and sent a covering note with the copies. This covering note has survived— Polycarp's letter to the Philippians—and from it we gather that the church of Philippi maintained its "true love" and "steadfast faith" together with that fellowship in the gospel for which Paul had commended it.

7
Paul's Word for Today

THEN AND NOW

IT IS POSSIBLE to read the New Testament letters
as sources of information about the life and thought of
the first century A.D., and certainly they are very
valuable sources for this kind of information. But that
is not the primary reason why Christians read them.
They are first-century documents, of course, and so it
is necessary to have some idea of their historical setting
if we are to understand them properly. But they are
more than that: they are part of God's word to men and
women in the twentieth century, and our primary
reason for reading them today is that we may hear what
God has to say to us in our present situation.

We must learn to distinguish between those features
which are incidental to the first century and those which
have a permanent message for every Christian century.
The incidental features are of minor importance; the
permanent message is of the essence of these writings.
For example, we can appreciate Paul's intention in his

directions about women's head-covering in church (1 Corinthians 11:2–16) all the better when we know something about ideas and customs in this regard in his lifetime in the places with which he was most familiar. But in many respects these letters of his, like the Bible as a whole, are concerned with matters of unchanging moment—things that concern Christians today as much as they concerned Christians in Paul's day. And, as we have seen, Paul does not deal with these matters as a private individual but as an ambassador of Christ; his purpose was not to get his own ideas across to his readers, but to enable them to know more fully the mind of Christ. To such good effect, too, did he pursue this purpose that the more we read and think about his words today, the more we can discern the abiding authority of Christ behind them.

THE LETTERS TO THE THESSALONIANS

The Second Coming

What have the two letters to the Thessalonians to say to twentieth-century Christians? Much of these two letters is taken up with the Second Coming of Christ. Does this subject play much part in the thinking of Christians of our age, outside a few eccentric sects? The fact that this was the subject studied by the World Assembly of Churches at Evanston, Illinois, in the summer of 1954, suggests that it is of more than marginal importance. Since then the emergence and acceptance of what is known as "the theology of hope" (after the title of a work by the main proponent of this approach, Jürgen Moltmann) bear witness to the essential part which this forward-looking note plays in the gospel. And the fact that in our recitation of the creed we repeatedly confess our faith that Christ will come from the Father's right hand "to judge both the living and the dead" reminds us that it is an integral article of the historic Christian faith.

Yet it must be confessed that most western Christians pay little more than lip-service to the doctrine of the Second Coming. Those who treat it with obvious seriousness, to the point where it plays a controlling part in the day-to-day planning of their lives, are apt to be thought a trifle eccentric, to put it mildly, and to be classified as "Second Adventists". Yet why should it be thought eccentric to take one of the historic doctrines of the faith seriously? Partly, no doubt, because this doctrine has been brought into disrepute on account of the fanatical misuse which some good people have made of it. We hear from time to time of pious individuals or groups deciding, on the basis of certain numerical data in Daniel or Revelation, that the Second Coming will take place on a given date; they publicize their findings, and are proved wrong in the event. When they go so far as to sell their property and give up their employment in expectation of the Day, as sometimes happens, such conduct simply confirms the majority of their fellow Christians in the view that the Second Coming can be dismissed from their minds for all practical purposes.

But this sort of thing has been going on for centuries; some Christians of Thessalonica were behaving in this way in Paul's day. If we look at Paul's way of dealing with them, we may learn to distinguish between the proper use of the doctrine and its misuse, and so avoid throwing out the baby with the bath-water.

The Christian hope

Christ has vindicated his title to be the sovereign Lord of history, and as the Lord of history he is over-ruling its course so as to bring it to its true goal. That goal is "the manifestation of his presence" (an alternative rendering of the phrase in 2 Thessalonians 2:8 which is given as "his appearing and his coming" in the Revised Standard Version). He is always present with his people, but his presence will one day be universally manifested and realized. The precarious days in which we now live make it difficult for us to share the confidence with which William Temple predicted, in the earlier years of the twentieth century, that future ages would look back to the first two thousand years A.D. as "the early period of Church history". But no matter how our Christian hope is influenced by the world around us, Paul would have us aware of the certainty of our Lord's coming without being carried away by a conviction of its immediacy. He himself did not know whether he would still be alive or not when that event took place; he hoped that he would be, but he could not be sure. He was no fanatical fixer of dates. Nor did he normally use the apocalyptic imagery of 2 Thessalonians to portray the Christian's "hope of salvation". His main concern for himself was that he should continue faithfully with his appointed work so that, if the Day did come in his lifetime, he would not be caught unprepared and ashamed. And this was his concern for his converts too, that they might be found "sound and blameless at the coming of our Lord Jesus Christ" (1 Thessalonians 5:23). The Christian hope gave no countenance to slackers and spongers; on the contrary, it should serve as an incentive to Christians to do their duty diligently, to help those in need, and generally to commend the gospel by their daily lives.

At the same time, the Christian hope was an inexpressible comfort to the bereaved and distressed. God, who had raised Christ from the dead, would raise Christ's people from the dead as well. This "sure and certain hope" of resurrection and eternal reunion was firmly based on faith in one who had proved himself to be the conqueror of death. Pagan tombstones and letters of condolence of the first century A.D. provide eloquent illustrations of Paul's words about grieving "as others do who have no hope" (1 Thessalonians 4:13). The early Christians commended the gospel by the way they died as well as by the way they lived; their twentieth-century successors can do the same.

The conquest of evil

Christians and non-Christians alike have unmistakable evidence of the power of evil in the world today, evil so powerful that it seems to take on an independent existence and insist on working its terrible will in defiance of all attempts to restrain it. (In fact, this cosmic evil is all of a piece with the residual fragment of evil which many a responsible citizen tolerates in his own life because it looks so harmless.) Here too Paul has a message of encouragement. In 2 Thessalonians 2:3–10 he portrays the ultimate incarnation of evil, so unconscionable as to exact unconditional allegiance, yet so subtle as almost to seduce the elect. What hope can there be against such God-dethroning power? No resources of our own strength or wisdom will avail; but all evil, even in its most recalcitrant form, must at last disappear before the power of Christ's appearing. This was the faith that inspired Luther's lines:

> "And let the prince of ill
> Look grim as e'er he will,
> He harms us not a whit;
> For why? his doom is writ:
> A word shall quickly slay him."

We can do with such faith today.

Thus Paul presents the doctrine of the Second Advent with sound practical sanity, using it as a stimulus to Christian faith and love, and as a strong encouragement in the face of death and the power of evil. Christ has already conquered; but the fruits of his conquest have yet to be experienced in their universal fullness. To use Oscar Cullmann's language, D-Day is past, but V-Day is still future. Meanwhile we who live "between the times" not only know his presence with us here and now as Victor and Deliverer, but also hold fast the well-founded hope that the future—both our personal future and the whole world's future—belongs to him.

THE LETTERS TO THE CORINTHIANS

Christianity in pagan surroundings

"The Church of God in Vanity Fair" is the title suggested by one New Testament scholar for the first letter to the Corinthians. The situation which called forth Paul's correspondence with the Corinthian church is the kind of situation which tends to reappear wherever Christianity is introduced to an environment whose ethical standards are very un-Christian. We should expect, then, that the "power" of the Corinthian epistles would be appreciated especially where a Christian church is planted amid pagan surroundings, as was the case in Corinth. Converts will feel the pull of old customs and old associations, and will find it difficult to understand why some of them should be frowned upon. They see no harm in them; why should they be condemned as incompatible with their Christian profession?

What are their missionaries and teachers to tell them? Some will be disposed to draw up a set of rules which young Christians must follow. Paul would say that this will tempt them to fall back from grace and live under law. Others will sympathize with them to the point of suggesting that some of those old pagan customs are not so deadly after all. Paul would say that this will tempt them to treat the grace of God too lightly and spoil their Christian witness in the eyes of their former associates. Others will follow Paul's way, the way of spiritual risk; they will trust the Holy Spirit to enlighten the converts' minds and renew their wills by his enabling word, while they themselves will, in Paul's words, endure birth-pangs with these spiritual children of theirs until Christ is formed in them (Galatians 4:19).

Christian liberty to-day

But it is not only converts from paganism who need to feel the power of Paul's Corinthian letters. Mature Christians, living as heirs of a long and rich Christian tradition, may need to learn afresh the lesson of Christian liberty. Outworn taboos can be cherished as if they were fundamental principles of the faith. Old customs which served a useful purpose once are sedulously maintained just because they are old customs, although now they probably hinder the cause of Christ instead of helping it. The enlightened and emancipated Christian will not tolerate such bonds. But at the same time he will deal very gently with others for whom these things are matters of conscience; the claims of Christian charity must be respected as well as the claims of Christian liberty. The Christian, in fact, will make it his aim to be "all things to all men" in the nobler sense of that expression, adapting himself and his behaviour in all non-essential matters to the company in which he finds himself, so that like Paul he may "by all means save some". It is sad indeed if a Christian lets some petty thing in his manner or language or dress or behaviour stand in the way of his being a blessing to others, because for some reason they find it objectionable or perhaps just irritating.

Marriage and the family

In a day when old landmarks in marriage and family life are being removed, has Paul anything to say to us on this subject? Much more than is commonly supposed. Paul has had for too long a prejudiced press where women, marriage and family life are concerned. But while he leaves us in no doubt about his personal preference for celibacy, he knows that it is a way of life for which only one here and one there are called and fitted, and takes it for granted that marriage is the normal state for Christian men and women (as for humanity in general). He asserts that male and female are spiritually equal in God's sight, he lays down the same rule of chastity for men as for women, and shows a profound and (for his time) quite exceptional insight into the mutual expression, surrender and union of two personalities which are involved in the sexual act.

Christian unity

Those with a concern for Christian unity have always

145

found a ready-made watchword in Paul's indignant question: "Is Christ divided?" It is not difficult to imagine what he would say to us to-day as he viewed our ecclesiastical or theological divisions. "Why," he would ask, "should you call yourselves Lutherans, Calvinists, Wesleyans, Barthians and so forth? Luther, Calvin, Wesley, Barth and the others are servants of Christ through whom you found the way of faith or learned the will of God more perfectly. But why should you impoverish yourselves by following only one of them, when all of them are gifts from Christ to his whole church?" He would tell us, too, that an external uniformity is valueless in itself and will not deceive anyone; only where there is true heart unity between Christians can the spirit of separatism be overcome. He would insist that the one true church is that which is built of durable materials on the one true foundation, Jesus Christ, but that within that church there is a home for everyone who confesses Jesus as Lord. And perhaps he would add that in our insistence that we must conserve the values which we have found in our own particular tradition we are selfishly subordinating the cause of Christian unity to a sense of our partisan importance.

Apostolic succession

In the contemporary dialogue on Christian unity the issue of apostolic succession plays a prominent part. Where is apostolicity to be found? Paul's Corinthian correspondence has much to teach us in this

146

regard. Paul's own apostolic status was questioned, and he could not appeal to history to validate it as members of the Twelve could. It was a matter of public knowledge that they had been commissioned by Christ. But Paul could produce no comparable evidence for his commissioning. His detractors said that he had imagined it all—that a vision was no basis for a claim to apostleship. How then did Paul defend his claim? He insisted, for one thing, that the risen Christ appeared to him just as really as he did to the Twelve. But he appealed to facts within his readers' knowledge as the conclusive proof of his apostleship. During his ministry in Corinth they had seen "the signs of a true apostle" performed in their midst (2 Corinthians 12:12); they themselves were in fact the "seal" of his apostleship (1 Corinthians 9:2). He had discharged an apostolic ministry among them; that was sufficient evidence that he was a real apostle. It is apostolic service that proves apostolic status, and not the other way round. That is no doubt what Paul would tell us to-day: the apostolic ministry can be recognized where the signs of an apostle are manifested. What he would say about attempts to make the apostolic ministry depend on an impeccable pedigree may readily be imagined.

Christian stewardship

What have the Corinthian epistles to teach us about Christian stewardship and Christian giving? Much every way. "You are not your own," says Paul; "you were bought with a price" (1 Corinthians 6:19f.). It follows that all that a Christian is, together with all that he has, belongs to Christ. When the cause of Christ is in need, then, it can call immediately on the resources which Christians have in hand. "God loves a cheerful giver" (2 Corinthians 9:7), and Christians are expected to be cheerful givers. After all, generosity on their part is an inevitable response to the generosity of Christ in giving himself for them. If Paul could see how grudgingly some Christians give a little to the cause of Christ, after making liberal provision for their own comforts and luxuries, he would say that obviously they had never learned the lesson that the Macedonian Christians had taken to heart.

What made them give with such joyful abandon, not so much according to their means as beyond their means? "First," says Paul, "they gave themselves to the Lord"; they looked on their scanty resources as his property and not their own (2 Corinthians 8:5). And they did not adopt this way of looking at things under apostolic pressure; they did so by a sure Christian instinct, and they would have thought it incredible that Christians should behave in any other way. Paul would tell their twentieth-century descendants that if only they inherited a tithe of the spontaneous generosity of those Macedonian Christians, the financing of the gospel in the world of today would be revolutionized. The gospel, he would say (and he might well be surprised that we should need to be told it), has first call on the resources of Christian people.

Co-operation of all

But it is not only the stewardship of money that is an urgent question in the church of our time. Christians have other ways of contributing to the welfare and advance of the Christian enterprise. In some quarters much is being said nowadays about harnessing the resources of the laity in the service of the Church. In other quarters, of course, this constitutes no problem; there are some Christian communities in which the resources of the laity have been fully utilized all along. Paul might indeed be a little puzzled if we propounded this problem to him; the distinction between clergy and laity would be a new idea to him, and one that would make little appeal to him. And if he were told how the distinction works out in practice in many Christian communities to-day, he would probably revert to his favourite analogy of the body and its members, and ask how on earth anyone could expect a body to be healthy if one of its parts were left not only to perform its own proper function but also to take over the functions of most of the others. When the Corinthian church met for worship, he would remind us, every member came along prepared to make some positive contribution to the service; in fact, so many wished to take part that it was necessary to impose certain restrictions in the interests of seemliness and order: it would suffice if two or three "prophets" spoke at one service, and no one should say anything unless it was likely to be of real help to the whole company. There would be no need for him to impose restrictions of this kind on most of our church services to-day; rather, he would urge many more members of the congregation to "stir up the gift" which God has given them. But this admonition would not apply only to their part in the regular services of worship; the church is, or should be, active seven days a week, and not just for a couple of hours on Sunday. And in the life and witness of the church every Christian has a special contribution to make; Paul would tell us that each one, no matter how handicapped or diffident, has a contribution to make which no one else could make quite so well. Every member of the body has an important function to perform, and all should be co-operating for the good of the whole.

The power of love

If we asked Paul to put his advice in a nutshell for us, perhaps he would invite us to read the thirteenth chapter of 1 Corinthians again, and digest all that he told the Corinthians there about Christian love. The exercise of all our talents in meetings of the church, the most strenuous exertions in doing good to those in need, fidelity to Christ that is willing to face martyrdom sooner than betray his cause—all these things are excellent, and worthy of the Christian name, provided that the impelling motive is love. "I may speak every language, angelic as well as human, but if I have no love, I am simply a resounding gong, a noisy tambourine. I may be able to prophesy, I may understand all mysteries and every kind of knowledge. I may even have the highest degree of faith—faith that moves mountains—but if I have no love, I am nothing, nothing at all. Yes, I may even give all my belongings away to charity, I may go so far as to be burned at the stake, but if I have no love, it does me no good."

He would look at our efforts to bring relief to the hungry and rehabilitation to refugees and economic aid to other under-privileged people, and ask us why we do it. Is it done out of sheer love? Then it is worthy of Christ and assured of his approval. Or is it done in the hope that those who are thus helped will be less attracted by the appeal of a creed which we hate and fear? Paul would ask us to be honest with ourselves, to recognize and admit our true motives; we shall know then how far our best-meant activities measure up to the standard of the love of Christ. If "the love of Christ controls us" (2 Corinthians 5:14), then we shall not regulate or apportion our charitable activities with an eye to any advantage of our own. "You know the grace of our Lord Jesus Christ," he would say; let others rejoice "because of the surpassing grace of God in you" (2 Corinthians 8:9; 9:14).

THE LETTER TO THE PHILIPPIANS

The mind of Christ

The same lessons are reinforced in the letter to the Philippians. In it Paul inculcates afresh the graces of contentment, joy, large-hearted generosity of spirit, forgetfulness of one's own interests coupled with a genuine concern for the well-being of others, unity of heart and purpose. But all these graces are included in his appeal to his readers to have among themselves the mind which was manifested "in Christ Jesus" (Philippians 2:5).

It has been pointed out that at church congresses, ecumenical gatherings and the like there is a tendency for advocates of this or that course of action to claim confidently that they are expressing "the mind of Christ", without giving any indication of the criteria by which it may be known whether or not any proposal is in keeping with "the mind of Christ". But here, in Philippians 2:6–8, the criterion is laid down with all desirable clarity. If a course of action involves giving instead of getting, self-effacement instead of self-advancement, serving others instead of receiving service, voluntarily plumbing the depths of disgrace and dereliction if only God's purpose may be furthered in this way—then the mind of Christ may be recognized with some confidence, for that was how our Lord himself acted. Unity of mind is best achieved when each aims at reproducing the mind of Christ; true Christianity, in fact, is the cultivation and expression of the mind which he manifested in all his ways.

FURTHER READING

(a) On Paul

BORNKAMM, G., *Paul* (London: Hodder & Stoughton, 1975)

BRUCE, F. F., *Paul: Apostle of the Free Spirit* (Exeter: Paternoster, 1977)

DODD, C. H., *The Meaning of Paul for Today* (London: Collins, 1958)

DRANE, J. W.,*Paul: An Illustrated Documentary* (Berkhamsted: Lion, 1976)

GRANT, M., *Saint Paul* (London: Weidenfeld & Nicolson, 1976)

HOCK, R. F., *The Social Context of Paul's Ministry* (Philadelphia: Fortress, 1980)

HOLMBERG, B., *Paul and Power* (Lund: Gleerup, 1978)

HOOKER, M. D., *Pauline Pieces* (London: Epworth, 1979)

HUNTER, A. M., *The Gospel according to Paul* (London: SCM, 1966)

HUNTER, A. M., *The Fifth Evangelist* (London: SCM, 1980)

JUDGE, E. A., *The Social Pattern of Christian Groups in the First Century* (London: Tyndale, 1960)

KECK, L. E., *Paul and his Letters* (Philadelphia: Fortress, 1979)

LONGENECKER, R. N., *The Ministry and Message of Paul* (Grand Rapids, Michigan: Zondervan, 1971)

MALHERBE, A. J., *Social Aspects of Early Christianity* (2nd edn., Philadelphia: Fortress, 1983)

MARTIN, R. P.,*Reconciliation: A Study of Paul's Theology* (London: Marshall, Morgan & Scott, 1981)

MEEKS, W. A., *The First Urban Christians* (New Haven: Yale University Press, 1983)

MONTEFIORE, H. W., *Paul the Apostle* (London: Collins, 1981)

RICHARDSON, P., *Paul's Ethic of Freedom* (Philadelphia: Westminster, 1979)

ROETZEL, C. J., *The Letters of Paul* (London: SCM, 1983)

STENDAHL, K., *Paul among Jews and Gentiles* (London: SCM, 1977)

STEWART, J. S., *A Man in Christ* (London: Hodder & Stoughton, 1964)

THEISSEN, G., *The Social Setting of Pauline Christianity* (Edinburgh: T. & T. Clark, 1982)

(b) On individual letters

There are excellent volumes on the Pauline letters treated in the preceding pages in the series called Black's New Testament Commentaries in Britain and Harper's New Testament Commentaries in U.S.A. (London: A. & C. Black; New York: Harper & Row): on 1 and 2 Thessalonians by E. Best (1972), on 1 Corinthians by C. K. Barrett (1968), on 2 Corinthians by C. K. Barrett (1974), on Philippians by F. W. Beare (1973).

The New Century Bible (Basingstoke: Marshall, Morgan & Scott; Grand Rapids: Eerdmans) includes commentaries on 1 and 2 Thessalonians by I. H. Marshall (1983), on 1 and 2 Corinthians by F. F. Bruce (1971), on Philippians by R. P. Martin (1976).

The Cambridge Bible Commentary on the New English Bible (Cambridge: University Press) includes volumes on 1 and 2

Corinthians by M. E. Thrall (1965) and on Philippians and Thessalonians by K. Grayston (1967).

The Tyndale New Testament Commentaries (Leicester: Inter-Varsity; Grand Rapids: Eerdmans) include volumes on 1 and 2 Thessalonians by L. Morris (1956), on 1 Corinthians by L. Morris (1958), on 2 Corinthians by R. V. G. Tasker (1958), on Philippians by R. P. Martin (1959).